COBB'S FARM (DUE NORTH)

COBB'S 20 ACRE LOT

FAY FALLS

THE NANCY BELLE
ANCHORED ON LAKE HAWK

UNDERGROUND HUT

RON CREEK

THE SOUTH WOODS

PRIVATE, PARENTS KEEP OUT!

PRIVATE, PARENTS KEEP OUT!

Written and Illustrated by Austin Stevens

Yankee Books
a division of
Yankee Publishing Incorporated
Dublin, New Hampshire

DEDICATED TO
UNCLE THADDEUS

Here was a noble pig. He could
turn adversity to triumph and
ammunition into food.

Table of Contents

Foreword

The nosey visitor was turning through the layouts on the editor's table. "What's this?"

"It's Austin Stevens' book, *Private, Parents Keep Out!*"

"Hey, they built a tree fort."

"Sure did," agreed the editor (instead of saying "Hay is for horses," as Austin's or the visitor's mother would probably reply).

"Austin and his pals had a secret club," murmured the visitor, leafing through the pages of this unfinished book with increasing nostalgia and delight. "Did they have a code?"

"Of course."

"And write with secret ink?"

"Naturally."

By this time, I was reading the text, poring over the drawings, and drifting back through the years when I, too, was doing the things that Austin Stevens has captured so exactly in this book.

"Geez, we had an underground hut," I said. "But we didn't roof it over with poles and turf. I seem to remember that Bob Anderson's folks gave us some old carpet, and we covered that with dirt and stones, and someone found some linoleum for the floor."

Our club was a detective club; we thought of ourselves as a deputy FBI office. In those days, the G-Men were busting such bad eggs as Baby Face Nelson, Pretty Boy Floyd, and Machine Gun Kelly, and we were always looking for clues to robbers and other felons.

The tree fort that Joe Appleby and I had wasn't nearly so wonderful as the one Austin, Paul, Jerry, and Nancy constructed (and that boys and girls can build themselves, from Austin's plans). Ours didn't have a roof. But it was off in a little patch of woods near Bob Grover's house, and it was our "Place." I ran away from home at least once and spent the night there under the stars. I even remember being besieged there one time by rough characters who showed up and heaved malodorous missiles at us.

The coding device that our club used wasn't nearly as sophisticated as the one that Austin reveals here (we sent away for Little Orphan Annie code pins with our mothers' hard-earned box tops), but we *did* send smoke signals from our underground hut to far-flung outposts.

By now the reader may have gathered that at least one ex-boy had a pretty wonderful time with this book. It took me back to the days before television when we seemed to have a lot of time between school, chores, part-time jobs, the Boy Scouts, and Saturday mornings at the "Y," learning to swim.

The adventures of the Hawks and the Clinton Brothers and the River Rats took place in the beauty of rural New Hampshire, not the frontier between a white-collar suburb and the countryside in upstate New York, where I grew up. But *Private, Parents Keep Out!* describes what life was like right across the USA before *Sesame Street*. We may not have had *Batman* on the tube, but every house had a furnace with dials and fire doors that could become the conning tower of a submarine where we kids hollered out "Dive" or "Fire Number One," or the cab of a locomotive in which we hummed "Casey Jones" while we highballed down the Rock Island Line.

This is a book about how absolutely wonderful it was growing up free in the good old USA. And all the things the author/artist describes and illustrates will still be just as much fun today for the boys and girls who want to try them. There are some surprises, too. Although I became a navigator in the United States Navy, I never learned to use a watch in place of a compass. And I now see why my stilts were always letting me down.

Of course, some things have changed and probably for the better. Even though the girl in our gang, B.J., gave me one of her father's big cigars to smoke in our underground hut — with catastrophic results — she wasn't allowed to be a *full* member. Democracy progresses slowly.

Some readers will discover marvelous stunts that they never thought of doing or knew how to pull off. I, for one, want to follow Austin's tips and make a Frankenstein monster the next time Halloween rolls around. Others will recall shenanigans untried by the ingenious Hawks of Walpole, New Hampshire.

I can't recall our gang burying "treasure," but we did bury a "time capsule" stuffed with items that should amaze archaeologists of the future, choice relics of the Boys' Community that we implored Secretary of the Interior Harold Ickes to help us incorporate.

Alas, I don't have a secret map to locate that buried time capsule. But no matter. *Private, Parents Keep Out!* is my time capsule. It's all here.

Robert Emmett Ginna, Jr.

CHAPTER ONE
In the Beginning

I Meet Paul

PAUL GALLOWAY AND I FIRST MET IN the summer of 1936. My mother had driven me to his house, promising me that he was "a nice boy," and that I would like him "just fine." But my mother had been so wrong concerning my social life in the past that I was quite prepared to dislike him from the start.

Introductions were made outside the Galloway house by our mothers — who having accomplished this simple diplomacy, dove into their own grown-up conversation, which had something to do with a cake sale.

Paul and I stared at each other — sizing each other up. I was six years old, and he was seven, Having never met anybody outside the family who was a full year older than myself, I was certain he'd take a poke at me as soon as our parents were out of sight. Because my older brother and two older sisters were forever taking pokes at me, I just assumed that the habit of smashing somebody for no reason at all was something that came on with age. As the doors closed behind our mothers, I braced myself for a fierce onslaught.

Instead, he asked, "Want to see my crow's nest?" We walked on down the dirt road by his house, a sun-dappled tunnel of green and gold, with maples on either side touching branches overhead. It's a tar road now, but in those days, grass grew in the center. We had walked about 300 yards when Paul stopped before a big maple tree. "It's up there," he said, "Can you climb trees?"

Although I never *had* climbed a tree, I didn't know that I couldn't, so I said, "Yes." Up he went like a monkey, and I followed, doing everything exactly as he was doing. Even when you're six, you know when you're being tested.

About two-thirds of the way up the tree, we came to his "crow's nest." It wasn't a crow's nest at all — just an old board nailed between two branches that forked from the trunk and faced a mighty view. As far as I was concerned, it was a brilliantly executed idea and a masterful piece of engineering.

So, we each passed the other's test. He didn't belt me, and I climbed up his tree.

YOU CAN BUILD A CROW'S NEST

First find a tree with two branches that fork evenly out from the trunk. (If one branch is higher than the other, your seat will be uneven.) Then you'll need a board about ten inches wide and long enough to span the two branches, and six three-inch nails. Place the board as shown and nail solidly to each branch. If you can do *this* project, you can do anything in this book.

I Meet Jerry

BEFORE SCHOOL BEGAN THAT YEAR, my mother had another fellow for me to meet. His name was Jerry Hamill. It was the same setup as with Paul. One morning over at the Hamills' house, our mothers introduced us to each other and started talking about cake sales at the church. Jerry and I were stuck.

"Want to go out in the forest?" Jerry asked. I had never heard woods called a forest before, except in fairy tales. But then, I had never climbed trees before either. Jerry had just moved up from Connecticut and had never been in either woods *or* forest. That's why his first step was to get a kerosene lamp from the horse barn and light it.

"What are you doing that for?" I asked.

"Because," said Jerry gravely, "forests are very dark." Still, it was only eleven in the morning and we were lighting a lantern to walk in the woods?

Jerry and his two brothers led the way, Jerry striding before us, his lantern held high. And through the sunlit meadow, we headed boldly for the dark wood. I couldn't help but admire his style. Still, he had *so* much to learn.

Now I had two friends. Paul was all country. He could do everything most country kids could do and much more.

TWO CHAIRS
CAN MAKE
AN INDOOR
HOUSE.

Jerry was up from the city, and as for country matters, he didn't know how to pound sand. But he was an intelligent lad and a willing worker. What I learned from and with these two in seven years of companionship could never have been learned in a classroom or from a parent.

For the first few years our projects were pretty simple, but fun. You know, things like piling two easy chairs on the floor on a rainy day to make an inside house — that is, your own house inside your family's house.

The Galloways used wood for heat. Their cellar was always full of wood. The wood was just chucked down the bulkhead stairs and then thrown into an area the size of a small room. Paul, Jerry, and I would stack it and make a maze full of alleys and secret rooms. This we would do in January, when the day was too cold or blizzardy for us to venture outside. Even then, I suppose, we were trying to find our own secret world, separate from our parents.

But as a working team, we didn't really get our act together until we were all around eleven years old. That was in 1941, the year Paul's eight-year-old niece, Nancy, came to stay at Paul's house.

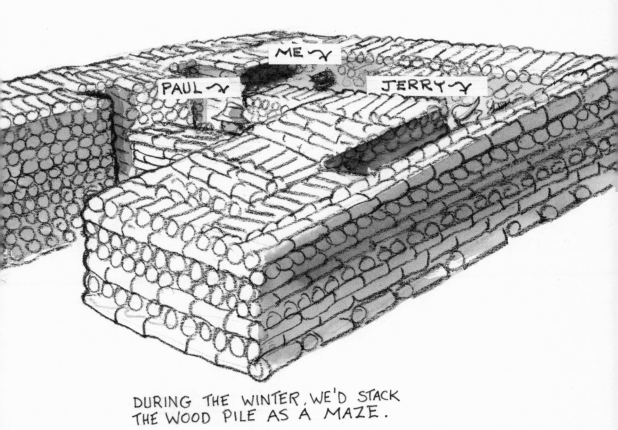

DURING THE WINTER, WE'D STACK THE WOOD PILE AS A MAZE.

17

CHAPTER TWO

The Tree Fort

A BLOCK OF WOOD NAILED TO THE DECK TO KEEP LADDER FROM SLIPPING.

SUSPENSION CHAIN

A Place

TO THIS DAY, I BELIEVE THAT THE LOSS of a single softball game provided the inspiration. Paul, Jerry, and I had long been friendly enemies of the Clinton Brothers. Actually, we weren't all that friendly with them, but we certainly did compete with them.

One Sunday afternoon, the Clinton Brothers whumped us good at softball in the field above Paul's house. After the game, when we were sitting around being discouraged, Paul made a decision. "We need a place," he said.

"What do you mean, a place?" asked Jerry.

"A *place*, you know," said Paul with some irritation. "A *place*-place; our place. A fort. A tree house." We were all silent, digesting this. It was certainly an idea.

Paul and I had built a Place before — a grain bag house whose life span would be measured in days. Not long after we finished this modest structure, late in the summer of 1938, the hurricane hit New England like a fist from hell. After the first hour of the storm only the wires of the frame remained, humming a mournful tune in the wind. In protest, I like to think. With this failure behind us, I had some doubt as to our ability to handle this new project.

"I've picked out a tree," Paul was saying. "Come and see it." He walked through the woods for about half a mile to Christian Hollow. We stopped at the ridge called Black Jack's Bluff. On top of the bluff, overlooking a field and a stream, stood a magnificent maple tree. Brawny, knobby branches sprang from its trunk like the great arms of a giant. Its best face looked east down on Cobb's Field across Cameron's Creek to Fay Falls.

"That *is* a tree," said Jerry, in awe.

"Then, are you with me?" asked Paul. We allowed as how we were.

Choosing a Tree

Paul was right to find the proper tree before even mentioning the Place project to us. Even your favorite climbing tree is not the best place for a Place unless it is Big — the bigger the better, with a strong series of relatively even branches. Look for a tree with three branches at least eight inches in diameter, or two branches at least ten inches in diameter, growing out from the tree at about the same level above the ground and reasonably close together. Ideally, the branches should be like the fingers of your hand when stretched wide apart. Your tree should be alive. That may sound silly but some of the most tempting trees we ever discovered were dead. A dead tree is dangerous to climb, let alone to build on. The branches are dry and brittle, and even big branches can snap off beneath your weight, suddenly and without warning. In June, you can easily tell the difference between a dead maple and one that is alive. A tree with leaves is alive; a tree without leaves is most certainly dead.

The tree wood should not be too hard. Soft wood is easier to hammer into, but the softest, pine, is full of pitch. Oak is really *too* hard. A maple tree is just about right, and its shape and limb structure lend themselves well to a tree house or tree fort.

The location of your maple is very important. If it's anything over a mile from your house, lugging wood and tools to the building site will be an agony. Still, if it's too close to the house, it's too close to civilization. The very nature of a tree house is *escape . . .* from parents and from the humdrum world of adults in general. A tree house built in your own yard is somehow not a tree house at all.

We didn't really have a distance problem because in those days I had a pony named Spotlight, also a two-wheeled vehicle we called "The Chariot." Spotlight was the nicest, most patient lady I've ever met. She was so well trained that all I had to do was think "Left," and she'd turn left. Riding her required as much concentration as walking on my own two legs. Spotlight was a good saddle pony. She was bridlewise and perfectly willing to pull a cart without panic. We used *her* to lug our stuff to the building site.

PAUL'S DOG: HIS FULL NAME WAS MUTT AND JEFF. WE CALLED HIM "JEFF" FOR SHORT.

Getting Lumber

While there are lighter building materials like wire and grain bags, we wanted something more lasting. Short of brick and stone, we recommend wood. If you have a wood lot, you can cut your own wood, but that is a *lot* of work before you even start to build, so scrap lumber is your best bet.

If you bought boards at a lumber company for the tree fort like the one we built, that would cost today in the neighborhood of five hundred dollars. Those are big bucks . . . even for your parents. And if you do get them to spring for that money, you'll end up with another problem. They'll want to build the house with you, and then it probably *will* end up in your back yard. No fun in that.

Go out and ask your neighbors if they have any scrap lumber lying around that they don't need. Every garage or barn is apt to have a few pieces of wood lying around. A board here, a piece of plywood there, perhaps even a rickety old shed somewhere that needs taking down anyway.

Visit building sites. Go right up to the contractor and tell him you're looking for leftover wood to build a tree house. He'll probably have at least one pile of small leftover stuff: two-foot lengths of boards or two-by-fours fit only for firewood — or tree houses. And if he decides he likes you and your project, he might dig up something really terrific.

One contractor told Paul and me, "I'm afraid I overbought on this building project, and the owner's coming around tomorrow. If he sees that pile of wood over there that I haven't used and never should have ordered . . . well, now — you can believe I'll be in trouble. Of course, I could hide it, but then, I don't have the time. But I certainly wish it were gone."

By 3:30 that p.m. — you can believe me, it was gone.

To build anything, you need structural timbers — that is, strong pieces of wood of proper length. Two-by-fours are perfect. A two-by-four is a piece of wood approximately two inches thick and four inches wide. Structural timbers will be the very bones of your tree house's anatomy. Everything else will be tacked onto these timbers. With them, you can make a skeleton called a "frame." You'll have to make one frame for the floor, and then others for the walls. What you tack on to the wall frames can be any kind of junk lumber — scraps of small boards, table tops, old doors, spare pieces of plywood, even linoleum. But the deck or floor should be *wood*.

I HOOKED UP SPOTLIGHT TO
THE CHARIOT AND THE WHOLE
BUNCH OF US HEADED OUT.

...AND THAT NIGHT WE DREW UP OUR PLANS. THAT IS, PAUL TOLD ME WHAT TO DRAW AND I DREW IT. JERRY AND NANCY MADE SUGGESTIONS. ON THE FOLLOWING DAY, WE WENT TO WORK.

WE HAD TO BRACE THIS CORNER

START BUILDING THE VERY NEXT DAY.

JERRY IS CUTTING OUT THE DEAD WOOD AND OTHER BRANCHES THAT WILL BE IN THE WAY.

PAUL GAVE ME A LEVEL AND TOLD ME TO KEEP THE BUBBLE IN THE MIDDLE - AND TELL HIM WHEN IT WASN'T.

PAUL IS SPIKING THE FRAME TO THE TREE.

THE FLOOR FRAME IS MADE OF 2" X 4"(S)

NANCY IS IN CHARGE OF KEEPING PAUL SUPPLIED WITH NAILS: PAILS OF NAILS.

WE HAVE AN UNSUPPORTED CORNER HERE. WE DECIDE TO DEAL WITH THAT PROBLEM, LATER.

23

WE BRACE OUR FRAME AGAINST TWO TREES.

YOU'LL NOTICE MY KNEE ACTION, HERE.

NAILS

THIS IS CALLED A LAP JOI

FLOOR JOISTS

How to Make the Deck and Walls

Build a frame on the ground. Let's say you were planning to build just a modest deck four feet wide by five feet long. (You have already measured the space between the branches chosen, so that you know a deck this size will span this space and can be nailed securely to the branches.) Cut two four-foot lengths of two-by-four lumber and two five-foot lengths.

Lay these two-by-fours out as shown on a flat area of ground next to a building or a couple of trees. Using three-inch nails, nail the boards together at the corners as shown to make a frame. When you are nailing, brace the frame against the building or the trees so that it won't move while you hammer in the nails.

Next, measure the inside width of the frame carefully — it should be about three feet, nine inches if you're working with planed lumber. If you use "rough"

or unplaned lumber, it will be a little smaller. But let's stay with planed boards for now. Cut three more pieces of two-by-four to fit inside the frame, as shown — each about three feet, nine inches long. These pieces are known in the building trade as floor joists. Space them evenly inside the frame and nail each end of each joist to the frame. Now your frame should look as shown above. Get some rope and haul the frame up into your tree. Position it and spike it to the branches.

If your deck fits the branches just right, you will be able to use five-inch nails, set "toenail" fashion, which means you drive the nail at an angle from the middle of the four-inch side of the frame into the tree branch. Otherwise, if you must nail straight through the top of your frame into the branch, you will need eight-inch spikes. Toenailing is a tricky thing to do at first, but it does make a stronger bind than right-angle nailing and requires far less muscle power.

24

Next you need some floorboards — one-by-sixes (boards one inch thick and six inches wide) are excellent — or pieces of plywood. Boards should be at least one inch thick, and plywood at least ½ or ¾ inch thick. The floor pieces should, of course, be at least four feet long. Nail your floor boards over and at right angles to the floor joists across the four-foot side of the frame. You can, if you wish, cut all the floor boards to their proper length on the ground — and then nail them onto the frame and floor joists. Or, you can take random lengths, nail them on as shown, and saw off the overhang all at once.

Once you have your deck or floor made, you can build on to it. The next step is walls. Again, build a frame for each wall on the ground, then haul it up into the tree with ropes. It's really quite like an old-time barn raising.

25

MEANWHILE: WORD REACHES THE CLINTON BROTHERS THAT WE'RE BUILDING A TREE FORT... AND THEY DON'T LIKE IT...

The Finishing Touches

To preserve the wood and keep your fort from rotting, you should paint it all. Getting old paint or stain is easy. Everybody always buys too much paint. In every garage or cellar in the country is a can, or cans, of old paint: crusty, stiffened, dreary old cans of paint. Most home owners are happy to get it out of their way, if you ask for it.

Make sure you know the difference between oil paint and latex. Collect only one or the other. Read the labels on the old cans or ask their donors. Whichever you have found the most of — oil or latex — mix it all together. You'll probably need to add some linseed oil or turpentine to old oil paint, or some water to old latex paint, to be able to mix it. By the time it is all mixed together and smooth, Paul's and my guess is, it will probably come out a sort of brownish grey "gunk."

Slap that gunk all over your tree house. It will hide everything. And, if you've followed these instructions exactly, you'll have a lot to hide.

27

A TARZAN SWING

If through luck or careful selection, you found a tree in a gully and there's another tree nearby with a high branch strong enough to carry your weight, you can develop an easy access to your deck or tree house. All you need is about thirty feet of rope at least one inch thick, which you tie to the branch overhead with a bowline knot. The nice thing about a Tarzan swing is, you can leave the same way you arrived.

START HERE

YOU MADE IT.

A STIRRUP SWING

Every real country kid thinks *he* invented this variation on the Tarzan swing. I'm sure *I* did. Again, the stirrup swing is basically a rope hung from a strong branch extending from the near top of a tall tree, but it is a little different from the Tarzan swing. For one thing, it's more for fun than access. For another, at the rope's bottom you tie a stirrup — either English or, if you're lucky, Western. Actually, either will work just fine.

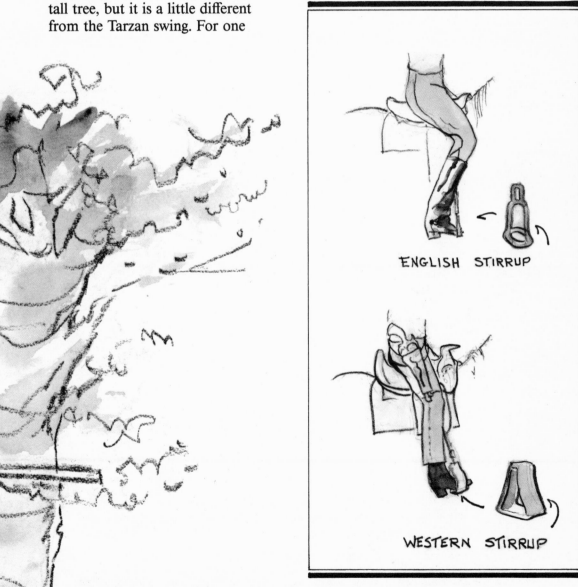

ENGLISH STIRRUP

WESTERN STIRRUP

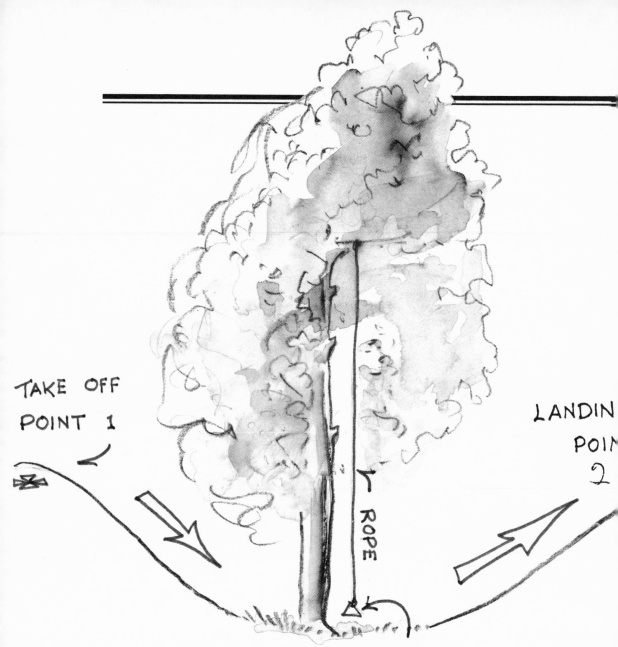

TAKE OFF
POINT 1

LANDIN
POIN
2

ROPE

STIRRUP

For a stirrup swing, you need a tree that stands in a little valley, with banks or hills on both sides. Find your tree, hang your rope from the high branch with a bowline knot as you would for a Tarzan swing, and then tie the stirrup to the ground end of the rope with a square knot, so that the base of the stirrup is about a foot off the ground. Now, test the strength of the knot and tighten it at the same time by stepping in the stirrup and lifting up, then dropping your weight back on to the stirrup. Lift your weight by pulling yourself up on the rope. Drop your weight by relaxing your hold on the rope.

30

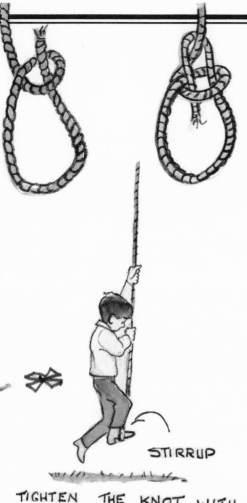

THE BOWLINE : THIS IS A GREAT KNOT TO USE FOR ANY SWING. ITS LOOP WON'T SLIP.

STIRRUP

TIGHTEN THE KNOT WITH YOUR OWN WEIGHT.

LIFT OFF.

AND AWAY!

Do this for about three or four minutes, at the same time noting how much the branch from which your rope is hung gives or bends under your weight. When the knot is tight, your weight in the stirrup should bring you within nine inches of the ground.

Carry the stirrup with you to Point One. Slip your right foot into the stirrup, bend your right knee, grasp the rope with both hands, stick your left leg out straight in front of you, and take off. In no time at all you'll be landing at Point Two! Do the same thing in the opposite direction, and Presto! you're back where you started.

CHAPTER THREE
A Secret Club

THERE'S LOTS OF HOCUS-POCUS IN A GOOD MEETING.

Getting Started

IF YOU HAVE A GROUP OF FRIENDS that always seem to be doing things together, sooner or later you're going to want to start a secret club. Secret clubs are very important because they provide privacy. Privacy develops when you have a secret place to meet — a "Place," as Paul said. That's most important. It can be a tree fort, an underground hut, even a bridge somewhere that you can crawl under.

In the early days Jerry and I had such a bridge. Nobody looks under a bridge unless they've come to repair it.

There are two kinds of clubs. One kind of club is formed to exclude all the "bad" guys. Another kind of club is formed to keep out all the "good" guys.

The Rat River Bunch was such a club. They took that name because their families all lived on either side of Rat River. They were a shiftless pack of brawlers ranging in age from 14 to 18. All of them over 16 had old beat-up motorcycles, old Harleys and Indians mostly. Bill Thorn, their leader, was the worst of the lot. He rode a 1939 Indian.

33

BIG BILL THORN AND HIS BEST FRIEND.

SAUL ROGERS IN HOT PURSUIT.

He wore a belt with beads of colored glass all over it. When he wasn't beating on somebody *outside* his club, he was beating on somebody *inside* his club. They didn't have much purpose in life other than to drink beer, cuss, and make a lot of noise. Their club was designed to keep out anybody who had an idea, wanted to build something, or for that matter, was interested in doing anything at all but drink, cuss, and make a lot of noise. I'm happy to say those qualifications limited their number to only about ten of the scroungiest, meanest, dirtiest pack of side-winders in our township.

If the Rats had a goal, it was to one day fix Saul Rogers, our town cop. Saul Rogers had many goals, but high on his list of priorities was one day to fix the Rat River Bunch.

Your club will be a "good guy" club, of course.

A real clubhouse should have a lock on the door. Your secret club should have a flag or a "totem." A "totem" need not be a carved pole — it can be anything that binds your club together as members of a "family" — a family

you select. You also need candlelight and ritual. And a certain amount of hocus-pocus.

So get your group together in your club house, light a candle, and start the meeting. No secret club is worth a dime without a secret. Pledge your group to keep the secret. Then tell them a secret — even if you have to invent one. Watch their eyes grow wide.

You should also develop signals, secret codes, documents of importance, and invisible ink. Always seal your letters with hot wax. You should have something of value, like a buried treasure, and a map you share that shows exactly where that treasure is buried.

Run your meetings tight. Always collect dues. If people have to give a little *to* something, they respect that something more. More important, you'll have a treasury to draw on in time of need.

Have the minutes of last week's meeting read aloud by the club secretary to help you all remember what you decided at that meeting.

Here's how we went about it.

35

Four Things Every Club Must Have

1. A Name.

2. Documents.

3. Secret ways to communicate: invisible ink, codes, whistles.

4. A Hidden Treasure and a Map to that Treasure.

Choosing A Name

WE HAD A TERRIBLE TIME ABOUT THE name business. Nancy wanted to call us The Watkins Hill Gang. None of us liked the word "gang."

Jerry wanted us to be called The PAJN Group. "Get it?" asked Jerry.

"Yes, we get it," Paul said. "It's the first letters of Paul, Austin, Jerry, and Nancy. But we don't like it."

I came up with The Four Musketeers. They all actually booed at that.

Paul suggested, "How about Compass Points 4?"

More booing.

"The Indians," Jerry said, "used to name their babies by holding them above their heads. They would face north and chant." Here, Jerry's voice dropped a full octave, "*God of the North, Name This Child.*" Now, Jerry went on in his normal voice, "If nothing moved, they'd turn the child to the east and say: *God of the East, Name This Child*, and then if nothing moved they'd . . . "

Jerry was cut off by Paul, who, in his own deep voice, intoned solemnly, "*God of the South, Name This Club. We've got it, Jerry, we've got it. But,*" Paul added, "we don't want a name like Running Brook or Leaping Bear."

We were sitting on the fort deck looking east. Above us, two hawks soared in the clear sky — lazy hawks, tipping their wings against a sea of deep blue.

"The Hawks," said all four of us in unison. And so it was that from that day forward we were The Hawks.

Documents

DOCUMENTS ARE VERY IMPORTANT and will take several meetings. A constitution is a good start. Usually written in high-flown language, a constitution is a document that sets down what your secret club stands for. It should speak about your principles and describe how you will rule yourselves.

When an argument develops between any two members, how will it be settled?

When somebody wants out of the club, how will that be managed?

What about taking in new members — how will you do that?

Our constitution started out like this:

In the spirit of the Hawk — who forever reaches up and soars easily above everybody else on earth, and whose eyes are keen, whose wings are strong, and whose heart is brave, we dedicate ourselves.

Jerry had penned this prose and was reading it to us aloud. His mother wrote for *The Atlantic Monthly*.

"That's nice," said Paul. "I'm not sure what it means. But it's nice. Go on, Jerry."

Jerry went on.

And so, in tribute to the Hawk's proud, bold nature, we dedicate our own spirits that we may one day soar above the ground and lift ourselves, our hearts, and our minds above all worldly things, to fly free in heaven's azure sky.

We were all very quiet, digesting this. Then . . .

"Where did you get 'azure'?" I asked.

" 'Azure' is blue," said Jerry.

"We're *asking*, where did you get that *word*?" Paul said patiently.

Jerry didn't say anything at first. He dropped his head and looked down at his hands. After a long time he mumbled, "From my mother."

Paul, Nancy, and I all looked at each other. Jerry wouldn't look at anyone, just kept on staring at his hands. Finally, Paul spoke the only hard words I had ever, in my memory, heard him say to Jerry. In a husky voice, he asked, "Which is it, Jerry? Would you like to be with *us* or with your mother?"

"With you people," said Jerry wretchedly, still staring at his hands.

After that painful episode, the rest of our constitution was pretty down to earth for four people who wanted to fly above "all worldly things." Jerry wrote it this way:

1. We'll vote on things when there is an argument.
2. We'll keep our secrets.
3. We'll stick together.
4. We'll always be there to help each other.

"GOD OF THE EAST, NAME THIS CHILD..."

You sure could tell when Jerry was writing on his own! I did the artwork for the document, and Nancy did the penmanship. We met one night to sign our constitution. Paul took a candle and lit it. Tipping it, he let the liquid wax under the wick drip down in a puddle beneath our names. While the wax was still soft, he took a walnut from his pocket and pressed it firmly into the puddle of the hot wax, then lifted the nut off quickly before the wax hardened.

"Why'd you use a *nut*?" I asked.

"Our seal is in tribute to Jerry, here." Paul said. He slapped Jerry on his back and roared with laughter. "Jerry, you're a nut." I laughed, sort of, second, Nancy laughed a careful third, and finally Jerry laughed and slapped Paul on the back a shade harder than I should ever have dared.

So much for our constitution. There are, of course, other documents you could have: pledges, annual reports, diaries, even stock certificates and copies of secret codes. But Watch Out — the paperwork can get out of hand, and stock certificates and codes can be STOLEN! Which brings us to secret ways of communicating.

Invisible Ink

WHEN NANCY WENT OFF TO CAMP FOR a week, she wrote Jerry a letter. Jerry showed it to us, and Paul looked worried when he read it. "It doesn't sound like Nancy," he said. "Something's wrong." Both Jerry and I re-read the letter and agreed.

"Well, she's trying to tell us something," Jerry said. "Do you suppose it's in code?" With that thought in mind we read the letter again, all together. There weren't any numbers on it — nor an obvious set of code drawings we could try to break. It was a simple, printed letter. But it didn't sound like Nancy. "Why did she underline *hot*?" Jerry asked.

"Because it was probably *very* hot that day," I said. "She probably forgot to write the word 'very' before hot."

"No," said Paul, "Jerry has asked a good question. Let's heat the letter."

SIGNING OUR NAMES IN BLOOD WAS NEVER MY IDEA.

"Heat the letter?" I asked.

"Just let's try it," he said.

We got a candle and lit it, then passed the paper back and forth high over the flame. Like magic, words began to appear between the lines. Finally, we could read Nancy's *real* letter. That's what's called "reading between the lines."

When Nancy came back from camp, we asked her how she made the invisible ink. A girl in her cabin had shown her how. "You make invisible ink by squeezing lemon juice into a glass. Use the juice as ink, writing your message with a clean pen point, then send the letter to somebody who will know how to heat it."

"Lemon juice? That's all?" said Jerry.

"That's all." Nancy went on, "But I really didn't believe you guys would ever figure out what the word 'hot' really meant."

The best way to heat an invisible-ink letter is over a hot plate or an electric stove, just because they have more heat *area* than a candle has; a candle will work fine, but will take a little longer. Turn the stove burner up high, and hold the letter about six inches above the burner. Move the letter in a circular motion over the burner. If nothing appears in about thirty seconds, lower the letter about an inch and repeat the circular motion. Just be careful not to get the paper too near the heat source, or your message will go up in flames!

July 28, 1941

Dear Jerry,
    I am having a lot of fun here at Camp Pokatatoo. We are supposed to write a letter every day. Our counselor is a beautiful lady. She reads all our letters to help us with our spelling, she says. She is lots of fun and has a very strong voice. The food here is wonderful. Tell Paul and Austin I'll be home in 2 weeks.
Love,
Nancy

P.S. It is hot today.

Secret message (printed between the lines):

I HATE THIS PLACE! MY CABIN COUNSELOR IS A NURD! SHE SPIES ON US EVERY DAY. SHE IS UGLY AS A STONE WALL FENCE. SHE SCREAMS AT US DAY AND NIGHT. I THINK SHE IS PART OF THE NAZI PARTY. HAVE DADDY CHECK HER OUT WITH THE F.B.I. SEE YOU. LOVE NANCY
P.S. THE FOOD HERE IS TRULY AWFUL Jill

After we heated the letter over the flame, words developed between the lines. The words were printed and the secret message gave us another whole picture of life at Camp Pokatatoo. Nancy had used lemon juice to make invisible ink.

Codes Are Useful

AT SCHOOL, THE CLINTON BROTHERS would always hang around us, listening in on our conversations. In the mornings, at recess, and during lunch, they always managed to be somewhere within earshot — eavesdropping. So we never could talk to each other openly. If we wrote a note in class and had it passed on, if a Clinton didn't get hold of it, the teacher would.

Once, I wrote Paul a note saying I couldn't meet him after school because Miss Rosner, our teacher, was making me stay after for tripping Lard when he went down the aisle to pass out papers. Paul sent a note back saying he'd come rushing in and tell Miss Rosner my father's house was on fire and my father wanted me home immediately. "That way," wrote Paul, "she'll have to let you off."

Well, Lard Clinton intercepted the note and passed it on to Miss Rosner. That afternoon, both Paul and I stayed after school.

"We need a code," Paul announced later at the next meeting of the secret club of the Hawks.

"Hear, Hear," we all said in agreement. There was scattered clapping.

"The whole trouble with a code," said Jerry, "is there never was a code that couldn't be broken."

"Miss Rosner isn't about to waste *her* time trying to break our code," said Paul with some irritation.

I piped up, "But the Clintons will."

"The Clintons," Paul answered, "are so dumb, they think the *English language* is written in code. Look at Ebon,

JERRY POLISHED HIS NAILS...

who's fourteen and still in Nancy's third-grade class!"

"How about we send away for a Captain Marvel Decoder Pin?" Jerry asked.

"Because," said Paul, "everybody else has one, including Miss Rosner."

"*She* didn't send away for one," I said. "She confiscated it from Harvey Stilton, who was supposed to be studying. Instead, he was sending coded insults to Marion Primm."

"Let's hear it for Harvey Stilton!" Jerry shouted waving his arms above his head.

Paul ignored Jerry's outburst. "Now, I've worked up a little code here," Paul said. "Let's see if you people can crack this!" Paul drew from his hip pocket a folded piece of foolscap. He unfolded it and pressed it flat before us. On the yellow paper were written these numbers ... 30/13/25, 9/25/21/23, 7/13/13/5, 13/25/23. Paul sat back, folded his arms, and went on, "You see even if you had a Captain Marvel Decoder pin you'd be lost with that code, wouldn't you?"

"I'm not lost," said Jerry. "I think I know what it means."

"*What?*" said Paul.

"You see," explained Jerry, "the two middle letters of the third word are both 13. That means they are probably two E's or two O's. The word is very likely LOOK. A 13 appears again in the first and last words, as well. As they are both three-letter words, we can guess the first one is YOU and the last one is OUT.

"Now we have YOU _____ LOOK OUT, which in fact, is all the message we need. Still, my last guess is that the second word, being of four digits, means MUST. Let me leap forward here and make a guess. I'd say the whole message reads, 'You Must Look Out.' "

Paul was very impressed. "How did you learn all this?" he asked Jerry.

Jerry polished his nails on his sweater. He then checked them for shine, pol-ished them again, and answered, "Well, I read a lot of Edgar Allan Poe. He was a fine code-cracker, you know." Jerry, at times, could be a real pain.

Ignoring Jerry, Paul said, "Here's the plan . . ."

Jerry cut Paul off. "Do you realize you can crack most codes by counting the symbol or number that repeats itself most often? Most often," Jerry went on, "that repeated letter is the letter E. And so, if you have a three-letter word that ends with E, you very likely have the word THE or ARE. After all, both are commonly used words.

"If you have been so observant that you have discovered this rather simple fact in your study of the code, you now have numbers or symbols for T, H, E, A, and R." Jerry thought for a moment. We all sat listening and learning. "And so," Jerry continued professorially, knitting his brows across his forehead, "if we can go this far with just one letter, the letter E, consider how very much further we could go with *five* letters."

I couldn't at that moment, speak for Paul or Nancy, but if either one of them had said, "Let's drum Jerry out of the corps," I would have gone along with them.

Paul was quietly writing out another coded message on a pad. "Let's you and me try this, Jerry." It looked like this: 30/13/25/40/9/25/21/23/40/7/13/13/ 5/40/13/25/23.

Jerry looked at it for a long time. "I don't think I could crack that one," he said, finally.

"Good," said Paul. Actually, as I reflect on things, I believe Jerry *could* have cracked it. He just knew when to leave well enough alone.

The upshot of that meeting was that we decided just one code wouldn't do. We had to have a machine that could offer us, quickly, many codes. The coding machine we worked out would give us more than sixteen different codes.

THE HAWKS' SLIDE-RULE CODE MACHINE

To make this foolproof coding and decoding machine (you'll want several), you need for each one:

A large sheet of poster board;
A jar of rubber cement;
Standard *lined* writing paper;
Exacto knife or matt knife;
Scissors;
Pencil or pen.

You're ready. Measure off and cut with the knife the following pieces of posterboard:

One piece 11 inches by 5 inches;

board (11 inches by 5 inches). It should look like this:

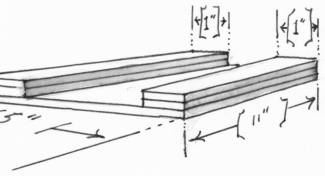

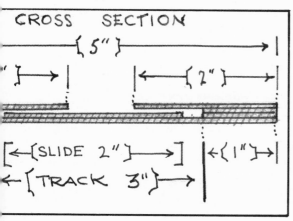

CROSS SECTION
5"
2"
1"
SLIDE 2"
TRACK 3"

Four pieces 11 inches by 1 inch;
Three pieces 11 inches by 2 inches.

With the rubber cement, glue two of the four pieces that are 1 inch wide along each outside edge of the biggest piece of poster

While the cement dries on that project, with scissors cut two pieces of paper from your ruled writing pad, each 11 inches by 2 inches.

Glue the two sheets of lined paper to two of the 2-inch-wide pieces of poster board.

When these two pieces are butted together lengthwise, the rules should meet exactly — as shown below. DO NOT GLUE THEM TOGETHER. You're just checking to make sure the ruled lines do line up with each other.

Cut from the lined writing pad another piece of paper 11 inches by 2 inches and cement that to the third piece of poster board that measures the same.

This piece is your slide. And its

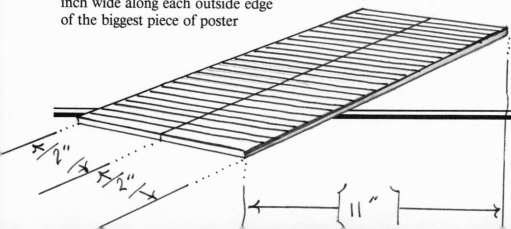

rules should line up with the other two ruled pieces. DON'T GLUE THEM TOGETHER! Just make sure they line up.

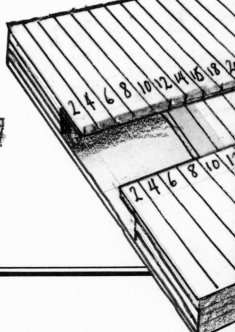

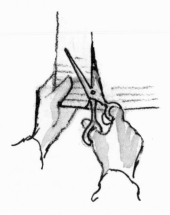

On the slide piece, letter the alphabet between the lines. On the two other lined pieces, write numbers in any order just as long as the numbers are in the *same* order on both pieces.

Place the lined, numbered pieces of board on top of the side pieces already glued down, so that the numbers on either side line up with one another. Make sure that the outside edges are even and that the ruled lines match up on both sides. Like this . . .

Now slip your slide into the slot and, behold, you have a coding machine that now has the potential of delivering and decoding no less than sixteen different codes. This should be enough for the time being.

Obviously, each member of your secret club should have his or her own slide-rule decoder. Even if the slide rules don't look exactly alike, they should *work* alike. Practice with them to make sure everyone has a machine that can communicate secret messages to the others.

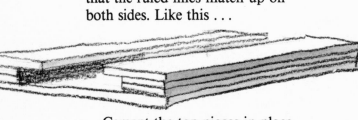

Cement the top pieces in place. Put a heavy book on top of the whole thing to press it while it's drying. Let dry for one hour.

Sending and Reading Messages

Here's how you use it.

Let's say Paul wants to send a message to Jerry. Paul must give Jerry the "key." Paul can write it like a date — *A/10/41* — which to the casual observer means April 10, 1941. But to Jerry it means that he should slide the rule so that the letter *A* comes under the number *10* on the decoder. The rest of Paul's message is nothing but numbers. With the slide set at A-10, Jerry can read the letter values for all the numbers in the message.

You won't always be able to use the date of the day you send the message, due to the limited length of the decoder. Just pick a date "key" that will give a number for each letter of the alphabet.

Pick a number that is not on your rule and make that mean a space between words. You've already discovered how easy it is to decipher a code if the words are separated, so rather than code a message so that it reads: 30/13/25 9/25/21/23 7/13/13/5 13/25/23, code it this way . . . . . 30/13/25/40/9/25/21/23/40/7/13/13/5/40/13/25/23/40.

Here the numeral *40* means the end of a word. Only you people will know this, so cracking that code will be a lot harder for everybody else.

Every time you send a new message — always put the new key in the upper right-hand corner, as you would the date on a letter. And if you have a free moment, you might type up your resumé (your background) and send it to the CIA.

They need people like you.

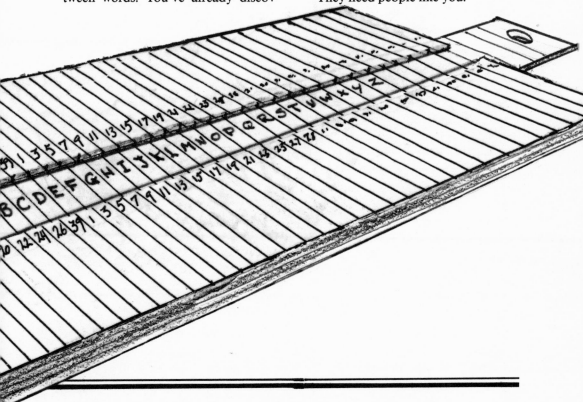

A SLIP-BARK WHISTLE

Each member of your club should also have a whistle to signal to each other in the woods or out in the open. Of course, you can *buy* a whistle, but those manufactured whistles all sound pretty much alike. If you build your own whistle, you can make your own sound.

You have to find the right tree for whistle-making. Some authorities recommend sycamore or willow. Some even recommend sugar maple saplings. Paul recommends *basswood*, and so did the Indians. Indians used only the sucker shoots. Sucker shoots sprout out from the base of the trunk of a basswood tree. To find the proper kind of tree, check the leaves. Cut off a piece of basswood (or sycamore or willow) 6 inches long and about 1 inch in diameter at the narrow (sky) end and about 1¼ inches in diameter at the fat (ground) end. Now your whistle is practically done, except for the following easy steps.

Make a cut all around the middle of your piece of basswood (or whatever), using a sharp knife and making sure to cut through both the outer bark and the inner skin. DON'T cut yourself instead of the bark. Then, with the same sharp knife, cut a slice off the narrow, or mouth, end on the diagonal. At

BASSWOOD LEAF

SYCAMORE LEAF

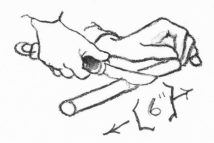

this same end, cut a window in the bark as shown.

NARROW END

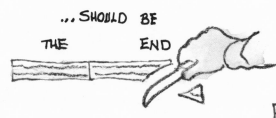

...SHOULD BE

THE END

NOTCH DOW

REMOVE THE BARK.

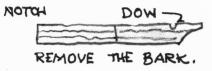

If you're in luck, the bark will slide right off the mouth end. If the wood isn't quite moist or young enough, you may have to tap the bark all around with a hammer. That should do it — if it doesn't, you have the wrong piece of wood. Slide the bark off the mouth end.

Now you should have two pieces that look like the picture. Next enlarge your "window notch" as shown. All you have to do now is slide the bark back on and give a toot or two. If you want to get fancy, put a screw eye in the end. Add a loop of twine so you can hang the whistle around your neck.

ENLARGE YOUR WINDOW, NOTCH.

RETURN THE BARK.

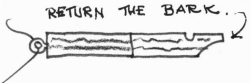

Finally, if you want to make your whistles work as signals for your gang, you should all learn Morse Code. If you really work at it, it will take you about an hour a day for a week. That may seem more than you want to get into, but just consider the edge your group will have on your opponents the next time you play Capture the Flag in the dark.

The Morse Code

A ·—	J ·———	S ···	2 ··———
B —···	K —·—	T —	3 ···——
C —·—·	L ·—··	U ··—	4 ····—
D —··	M ——	V ···—	5 ·····
E ·	N —·	W ·——	6 —····
F ··—·	O ———	X —··—	7 ——···
G ——·	P ·——·	Y —·——	8 ———··
H ····	Q ——·—	Z ——··	9 ————·
I ··	R ·—·	1 ·————	0 —————

48

Treasure

AFTER OUR CONSTITUTION, PLEDGES of allegiance, and other important documents were completed, we decided we should bury this material.

We put all the papers in an old tin cigar box Paul found. We decided that we should each put something of value to us in the box as well. The mix of "valuables" was highly personal and somewhat strange. I put a set of carved bone "HEAR NO EVIL, SPEAK NO EVIL, SEE NO EVIL" monkeys in a change purse and offered it to the box. Paul contributed a German soldier's belt buckle with a rather sinister-looking eagle stamped on it. Beneath the eagle were the words "Gott Mit Uns," which I later learned meant "God's with us."

Jerry brought a fishhook with a hand-tied fly. "It's a Royal Coachman," he told us. "My father tied that fly." And Nancy brought a broken Mickey Mouse wrist watch with a cloth strap. With his hour hand broken off at the elbow, and only one eye, Mickey looked even less friendly than Paul's German eagle.

Everything was stowed away in the tin box and that night we buried the treasure in Christian Hollow. Its place is marked on our map. We didn't really need the map because Jerry had developed a little poem that we all memorized. It went like this:

Left of the maple, north 23,
And south of the old oak tree.
Four steps west of the hanging branch,
And there you'll find our treasure to be.

I couldn't help but wonder if Jerry's mother wasn't writing his stuff again.

CHAPTER FOUR
Halloween

I HAD THE FEELING I
WAS BEING FOLLOWED...

PAUL AND I DIDN'T LIVE IN THE town of Walpole. My family lived on Watkins Hill, and he lived on County Road. Both houses were about four miles out of town.

A school bus picked us up in the morning and delivered us back to our homes in the afternoon. Often, he would ask me to get off at his house, telling me about some great new project he was working on, so that *not* getting off was always an impossible idea.

Perhaps in the long run I would have done better for myself if I had simply ridden on home and done my homework. But I was never really into homework. I'd get off with Paul instead.

The tough part came when it was time to go, because I had to hoof it. It was about a mile between our houses as the crow flies. And the way was along an abandoned road through dark woods.

In the fall of the year that lane was pretty spooky. From Paul's house to mine, it rose gradually in elevation. At the crest of the hill, about halfway home, the dark woods gave way to apple orchards on both sides. The night sky could make a fierce show of flying clouds. On such a night, the moon was always on again, off again, as the clouds flew over it.

When the moon stood behind rolling clouds, the path was dark as lampblack. But when the moon came out again, the path was bright as day.

Still, even when the land glowed silver in the moonlight, there were dark shadows criss-crossing the lane — shadows that rippled and moved beneath my feet. The wind was always high on that knoll, and the apple trees would creak and wave their boney arms and fingers at me, while pine trees rocked like great, black dancing bears, their needles keening in the wind.

Walking home one mid-October night, I got the notion someone was following me. Of course, when you're eleven years old, it's someone OR . . . . . *something.*

Four times in about two hundred yards, I wheeled to see if I could catch a glimpse of my stalker. Always, I thought I had just barely caught sight of him as he ducked behind a tree or a ragged stone wall. He had to be a giant imp, toying with me — cat and mouse.

I felt cold all over and a tingling on the back of my neck. I looked for a big stick to carry and eventually found one. It was a weapon to wield, if wielding weapons became necessary. Funny. In the very act of doing that, I quieted down.

Nothing, I concluded, was behind me except my own imagination. Still, one's imagination can be one's own best friend . . . . . or, one's own worst enemy.

I decided right then to put mine to good use and have one very scary Halloween party.

A Halloween Party

IF THERE IS ONE SPECIAL DAY OF the year that belongs to the young, it's Halloween. If you're planning a party — a real Halloween party with tricks and props and scary stuff all over the place, you had better plan to chain your parents upstairs, or in the kitchen, or out in the garage. You could lock them in the cellar — whatever is your style. But get them out of the way. No friend of yours is going to feel afraid of anything if there is an army of parents hovering around.

Get permission to use a section of the house that will be free of grown-up traffic. If you can get the front hall and one large room, or even better two rooms, you're all set.

The large room is the party room. Your mother can be of great help there. Doughnuts on strings and bobbing for apples are traditional Halloween games, and she will probably have lots of good ideas for Halloween food: devil's food cake, a witches' brew to drink, and so forth.

Decorate that room with the standard Halloween decorations — lighthearted pumpkins, happy dancing skeletons, snarling black cats — and have colorful paper plates and cups.

The *other* room is all your own — name it what you will. Call it HALL OF HORRORS, THE DEVIL'S CAVE, or whatever, but make sure it is *very dark*.

At some point in the evening, your friends will have to pass through that room and face horrors they never dreamed existed: the Frankenstein Monster; a Bloody Head on a Platter (moaning); a Real Black Cat; Bats in their faces; a Witch Boiling a Pot of Worms (and tasting her stew with a wooden spoon). And finally, they will have to pass through the Curtain of Snakes.

As they approach each exhibit, a strong light is suddenly directed at it. The rest of the room is still *very dark*. First they will see the Frankenstein Monster, seven feet tall. Suddenly, he surges toward them, growling and screeching, waving a bloody ax over his head. The light goes out. They grope through the dark again, when suddenly the light is turned on and directed at a table. On the table is a bleeding, severed head, resting on a platter, moaning warnings for them not to go on.

And so forth.

If you do this really right, everybody in your party is going to have a premature heart attack. It is my sincere hope you will botch up enough of this so nobody will be terminally terrified.

A MONSTER

This is a project that a whole group can work on together, separately. Divide up the work so your gang's artist does the head, your best carpenters build the body structure, and your best costume designer takes care of the costume.

We felt it was important that the Frankenstein Monster be able to rush at people. Paul said he ought to be carrying a bloody ax, but Nancy worried about the ax falling on somebody. Jerry felt that that would be okay if it fell on one of the Clinton brothers. In the end we left it up to Paul.

I was chosen to do the head, Paul and Jerry would build the body, and Nancy would make the costume.

A WALKING, TALKING FRANKENSTEIN MONSTER

The Head

Get a large roasting pan or washtub — anything large that holds water.

You need lots of newspaper or paper towels. Last week's Sunday edition of *The New York Times* should be plenty of paper. Also, get scissors, poster paints (including a pint jar of white poster paint), and a large round or oval-shaped balloon.

STEP 1

This is sloppy work, so find some indestructible surface — like the Formica counter top in your kitchen. It will take time, so don't start the project 30 minutes before supper time.

Cut about a hundred and fifty strips of newspaper 1½ inches wide and six to eight inches long. Next mix flour and water together in your large pan, using enough flour to make a mixture that is thick, but still fluid. Now submerge about fifteen paper strips in the pan of paste. Make sure the paste saturates the paper on both sides.

STEP 2

Blow up your balloon. Blown up, it should be about the size of a human head. Tie it off tightly with an elastic band.

Begin bandaging the head with soaked paper, strip by strip, until the balloon is completely covered with a double layer of strips.

Now, with shorter strips of soaked paper, begin to build up the shape of the monster's head. This will take time. You can speed up the process by bunching soaked strips and then covering them immediately with flat strips to hold them in place.

STEP 3

But don't hurry the job. A Frankenstein Monster should have a head fairly flat on the top, heavy brow, deep eye sockets, high cheekbones, and a strong jaw. When you've created these shapes by bunching and bandaging, let the head dry for 48 hours. Don't touch it or move it while it is drying.

When the head is dry, cut ears out of a piece of poster board or thin cardboard. Glue them in place with white glue (Elmer's glue is fine), making sure, of course, that they stick out a little from the head.

STEP 4

Break an old Ping-Pong ball in half along its seam by pinching it — now you have two eyeballs. Using white glue, paste each half of the Ping-Pong ball into an eye socket. Let the glue dry overnight.

Next day, paint the entire head white with poster paint. And if you need to, paint on a second coat to cover all the newspaper type. Let dry for one hour between coats.

Now paint the entire head with your chosen color — I recommend something close to your own flesh color but with a deadly, greenish tint. Then, using some color like pine tree green, draw in eyelids over the eyeballs so that the eyes are slits.

PIN

STEP 5

Paint in under the cheekbones — draw in the line between the lips. Paint the eyebrows and have fun.

When the paint is dry, puncture the balloon from the underside of the head and cut a hole big enough to stick the neck pole into.

You might consider using real hair for the monster's head. You can find that in abundance at any barber shop. Or use horse hair. Finally, glue two corks (simulating Frankenstein's spark plugs) to both sides of his jaw, just under his ears. Add stitches as shown. Beautiful!

Time to see how your friends are doing with the body structure and the costume.

STEP 6

PAUL DRILLS ALL THE HOLES FOR THE MONSTER'S FRAME IN ONE EVENING.

The Body

One way to build a body is to make a sort of scarecrow frame. Dress it, stuff the costume with old rags and newspapers, and just let it stand around.

Paul wanted a monster that moved, so he built a frame light enough to carry out of one-by-one (sticks one inch square) boards. He used ¼-inch nuts, bolts, and washers at the joints so that the arms could be moved and fixed to whatever position was wanted, once the monster was complete. The bolts were inserted into holes drilled into the frame, with washers under the top of each bolt and under the nut screwed onto the other end.

Even then, with an overcoat on, the monster would be heavy. So Paul got an old tomato can and hooked it to his belt with a wire. Flag bearers in parades use this sort of device. Their arms don't carry the weight of the pole and flag — their whole body does.

He bolted the arm poles to the ax handle (the ax head was made from two shingles). Jerry cut some old farm gloves and tacked them to the arm poles in position. Then they stuffed the gloves with old rags and sewed up the openings with needle and thread. (It took Paul and Jerry less time to do all this than it took me to make the head.) Last of all we placed the monster's head on the neck pole and glued it in place.

WASHER AND NUT.

T AND WASHER

WASHER AND NUT.

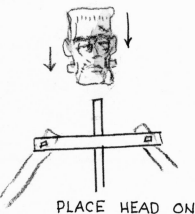

PLACE HEAD ON
STICK THROUGH
BALLOON HOLE

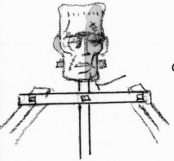

GLUE HERE.

PAUL'S FRAME

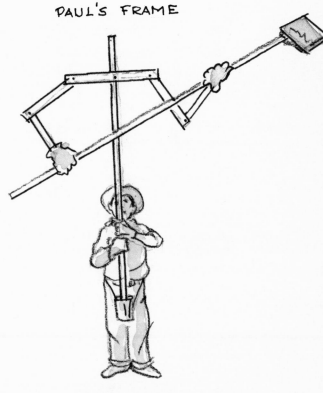

PAUL CARRIES THE
WEIGHT OF THE FRAME
IN A TIN CAN THAT'S
ROPED TO HIS BELT.

The Costume

Nancy's solution was the simplest one of all. She found an old winter overcoat of her father's in the attic closet. Her father was six feet two inches tall, while our monster was seven feet tall, but when Paul toted Frankenstein, the coat was long enough to cover most of Paul's legs. We put the coat on the monster backwards, and cut holes in the coat for Paul to see through.

GROANING HEAD ON A PLATTER

The groaning head is a lot easier. You can do everything except Step 1 below just before "Show Time." Just make sure you have all the equipment on hand.

1. Cut a hole big enough to put your head through in the top of a very big cardboard box. Drape the box with an old sheet, cutting a hole in the sheet to match the hole in the box. (You'll have to prepare your mother for the fact that the sheet will end up with a hole in it.) Get a

stool you can sit on comfortably when you are in the box.

2. Cut a large paper plate in half and cut half a hole from each side as shown. Insert your head through the hole in the box, and have a friend fit the plate around your neck like a collar. Cover the seam by spilling catsup on the plate.

3. Put on a tortured expression and get ready to moan when the light hits you. Wear a wig — Jerry did — and make up your face if you like.

A WITCH'S STEW OF WORMS AND PICKLED EYEBALLS

Take a package or two of spaghetti. Break the spaghetti strips in half and set aside. Get a pot — preferably a large, black cauldron, and fill it with water, then tint the water dark brown with a mixture of red and green (or blue) food coloring. About 20 minutes before the show, place the pot or "cauldron" on a hot plate, and let it come to a boil. Dump in the spaghetti strips. Turn the hot plate off. Put on a witch's costume and sit before steaming stew of squiggly things — sipping the stew from time to time. Whisper to your audience that "worms taste good, if they're properly seasoned." Use a wooden spoon and cackle a lot. Now and then offer them a spoonful of your cooking skills. Have handy an open "can of worms" (cooled spaghetti) and a jar of pickled eyeballs to hand out.

To make pickled eyeballs, just slit the skin of a grape and remove it. That's one pickled eyeball. Keep working at it, gang, you'll need 500 grapes to make a big glass jar look really dreadful. If there is a scoffer at your party, dare him to put his hand in the jar.

A CURTAIN OF SNAKES

Various lengths of yarn, string, or strips of cloth soaked in cold water or cooking oil and hung over a clothesline rope should do the trick. It should be very dark for this effect. Light should shine only on the sign that tells your friends what they are about to face. "YOU ARE ABOUT TO PASS THROUGH THE CURTAIN OF DEAD SNAKES (at least MOST of them are dead)." Have someone back-stage hissing.

And finally —

BATS IN THE BELFRY

Find some old inner tubes. From the rubber, cut out your standard bat (BATMAN) shapes in two or three different sizes. Cut out a lot of bat shapes. Hang them from the ceiling with black thread. Hang them everywhere and low enough so that your guests' heads keep banging into them. Understand, you want your guests to have a good time, but it is Halloween.

Make one huge bat with an 18-inch wing span out of black poster board, and call him DRACULA. Cut holes for eyes and backlight them with a flashlight. Hang Dracula up high, so no one will knock down the flashlight.

NANCY ANSWERS THE DOOR AND THE CLINTON BROTHERS GIVE HALLOWEEN THEIR BEST SHOT.

Rubber Bats

THE AWFUL CURTAIN OF SNAKES

E KES UTS, AND

BUT FIRST SAMPLE OUR STEWED EYEBALLS AND CANNED WORMS

LY CAT.

Spotlight

NS ON N THE S GO TAIN OF WILL BE POP!"

WE FINALLY DECIDE TO LET MY PARENTS WATCH, IF THEY WOULD PROMISE TO KEEP IN THE BACKGROUND. THEY DID . SORT OF... THAT IS, MOTHER KEPT HER PROMISE...

... ALL IN ALL, IT TURNED
OUT TO BE A PRETTY HORRIBLE
PARTY, WHICH BY OUR
STANDARDS MEANT THAT
IT WAS A GREAT SUCCESS!

CHAPTER FIVE
When Winter Comes . . .

ICE IS NICE.

BEFORE THE FIRST SNOW,
WE CLEARED THE AREA OF
LEAVES, TWIGS AND STONES.

A Skating Rink

BY THE MIDDLE OF DECEMBER, PONDS in New Hampshire are usually iced over. The first thin skin of ice appears around Thanksgiving. The ice isn't really safe to skate on for another week or two — by about the end of December. By then, it is often snowing. An inch or two of snow is easy to clear off with a shovel or a broom. But when January hits, you can get snowfalls that cover a frozen pond with a blanket a foot deep or more.

If there is a big wind up during a storm, it *may* sweep the pond clear of snow. But you can't count on that. More often than not, the snow just keeps on coming and gets way ahead of you, whatever you do. Even if you and your friends *do* manage to clear the

pond, the ice will be such a mess you'll find you've shoveled for nothing. By the end of January, your skating parties could be all over for the winter, unless you've built a skating rink.

Looking back on it, I guess the reason Paul, Jerry, Nancy, and I decided to build a skating rink out behind my family's barn was because my family had a pump-driven well that delivered 20 gallons a minute. You don't need all that much water though. You only need about the same amount it takes to sprinkle the lawn in August.

We started on the rink well before the first snow. This gave us the opportunity to clear a flat piece of land. We cut the tall grass down with a scythe and raked the leaves and twigs off the area.

66

AND AFTER THE FIRST GOOD
SNOW FALL, WE PUT ON OUR
SKIIS AND PACKED THE
WHOLE AREA DOWN.

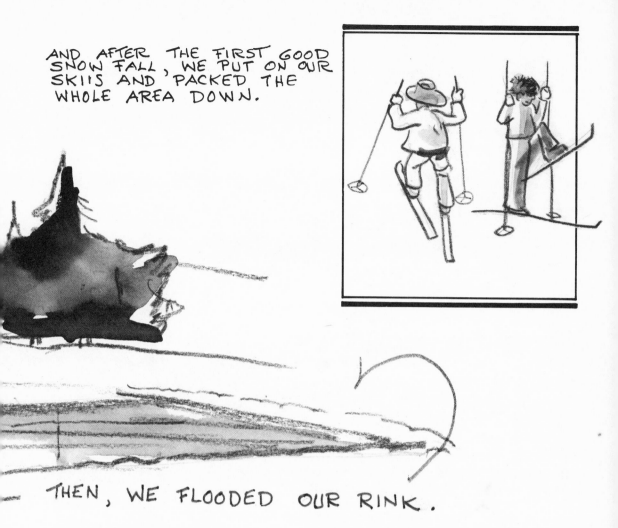

THEN, WE FLOODED OUR RINK.

The snow came late that year; we got a foot December 22nd. Which was lucky, because it takes a foot of snow to make an inch of ice. The four of us got out our skis and packed the snow down hard. It would have been better if my older brother had been around to pack the snow with our Model H John Deere tractor or if we had thought to use a lawn roller. But we did pretty well, stamping down the snow with our skis on, and later stamping down the high spots with just our boots. It took us four hours to pack the snow properly.

That evening we hosed, or "flooded," the rink for an hour. By the time we'd done that for four days in a row, we thought one more hosing would give us a surface of nice ice. We did that, then we planned a skating party. We had the skating party, but the ice was *not* nice. It was like skating on iced-over pebbles. Our skates chattered beneath us, but they helped the surface a great deal. The skate blades cut up the rough spots — actually chopped up the ice, so by flooding the rink again that night, we fixed it up just fine. The next day the rink was like a pane of glass — smooth and faultless. Perfect.

That night it snowed eight inches. As soon as the snow stopped, we shoveled it off, and found our surface was still like glass. Even if, by some weather quirk, the ice became a mess again, we knew that all we had to do was to flood the rink again. Keeping this up, we could skate from January to March.

67

AND WHEN YOU'RE NOT SKATING. . . MAKE A TRAY SHOOT

A TIN TRAY WILL MAKE A DANDY SNOW SCOOT.

Each winter is different. Some are full of snow, some are full of wind, some are full of both. Some winters go up and down in temperature, with warm days around 33 degrees Fahrenheit, and very cold nights in the tens, or roughly 23 degrees below freezing. If you luck out, you'll get a winter like that about every three years — perfect for building a tray shoot.

A tray shoot is an ice run. The trick here is to make the track by sliding down the hill before the crust has formed over the snow. Do it on your mother's favorite tray. Build up the corners, and

BUILD UP THE CORNERS SO YOU HAVE A BANK TO PITCH AGAINST ON THE TURN.

HELLLLLPPPP!

YOU MUST BE FEARLESS.

bank the curves. Let the track you made freeze that night.

During the day, the warm sun will soften the track, while the cold at night will freeze it solid again. If you hang in there, your tray shoot will get faster and faster. Your corners will get steeper, and your runs will get wilder. . . . And your mother will be furious. Mine was. You can't really blame her. I used the tray left to her by her very own Aunt Agatha!

(If you followed this advice, YOU'RE IN A HEAP OF TROUBLE, KID. Still, you've had a lot of fun.)

SNOW SCULPTURE

YOU CAN ALWAYS BUILD YOUR STANDARD SNOWMAN ... OR ...

For winters with lots of snow, snow sculpture is the thing. Make yours out in front of your house, so you can use a hose from the house to "freeze" your sculpture every night until you finish it. Most people build a snowman, stick two brooms in his sides for arms, and place a hat on his head. Then they stuff a piece of coal in the general vicinity of his nose, two more pieces of coal where his eyes should be, and that's their snowman.

You can do better. For instance, you people could do The Great White Shark. Build a high cone of snow ... put in two eyes, then carve a mouth, and ... Instant *Jaws*!

You'll scare the neighbors to death.

...EXERCISE SOME ORIGINALITY. BUILD JAWS! (OR SOMETHING LIKE THAT.)

Frozen Solid

DURING MARCH OF 1942, WEATHER AND temperature in our town of Walpole, New Hampshire, combined to create a condition I have never seen before or since. It had been a wild and snowy winter with five feet of snow piled up everywhere. In March it began to rain the way it *should* rain in April. The rain poured down without stopping for five days, turning the top two feet of snow into slush. Then all of a sudden the temperature dropped below zero and stayed there for another five days, Our world was crusted over with two feet of solid ice — over lawns, meadows, and woods.

On March 13th, I went skating with the Boy Scout troop on Kingsbury Pond. We horsed around on the ice playing Capture the Flag, Tag, and Snap-the-Whip. When it was time for lunch, some of us decided to "cut cross lots," taking a short cut home through the woods.

We walked, slipped, slid, and now and then fell on what looked like snow, but what was actually ICE. We held onto trees, crawled on our hands and knees . . . all the time howling at each other in sheer exuberance. Downhill we slid on the seat of our pants. The woods rang with shouts and laughter.

Then, all at once, we fell into this bowl-like pocket — a miniature valley, where we found ourselves prisoners of the ice. There were no trees to grab onto to pull ourselves up or to use as a ladder. Try as we might, time and time again, to escape that crystal prison, we could get just halfway up the wall, only to slide right back into the bowl again.

Then Charlie Dunbar, who had never displayed any great intelligence before (it took him three tries and a tutor before he could make Tenderfoot), solved the problem. He took off his shoes, laced on his skates, and walked up out of that ice bowl on the toes of his skates, driving in the blades with each step along the way. At the top edge of the bowl, he turned back to us, victorious! He waved wildly, laughed, then turned and shot down the other side of the hill. Down through the woods he sped, hooting and hollering, skating on snow. In and out and around the trees he went — now and then holding on to one, wheeling about it to change his direction, then letting go and skimming over the ice snow down the hillside and through the woods.

His was the only way out. Digging the toes of our own skate blades into the ice, we climbed out of the bowl and, as he had done before us, shot down the other side of the hill. We were all screaming and shouting at each other.

Now and then, somebody would fall. When that happened he was helpless. He would slip, slide, and cartwheel along flat on the ground, laughing all the time because even falling was fun.

We all raced home and told our friends and families. By 3:00 p.m. everybody in town who had skates was out on the ice snow, skating over lawns, hill tops, the golf course at the country club, through the woods and valleys — you could quite simply *skate anywhere*!

CHAPTER SIX
Put on a Big Show

IN THE WINTER, ALONG ABOUT February or March, a young person can get house-bound. By that I mean, stuck in the house. Your mother can get on your nerves, and, make no mistake about this, you can get on *her* nerves, as well. When the weather is so awful no one in his right mind would go out, you need something to do. Plan a theatre night. Make it a competition. Ask your friends to come up with a stunt or skit — you know, a short play, or a magic act, something entertaining — and offer a prize for the best act.

I volunteered my house for the big night and we sent an invitation to the Clinton Brothers — not just your usual invitation . . .

Big Academy Award Night

You guys are useless. You're not funny, you're not interesting, and you're not even entertaining. If you say you are, you'll have to prove it. Work up an act and be at Austin's house for free Coca-Cola and sugar doughnuts on February 8. That's 6:00 p.m. Be there on time. You might want to take a bath before you come. If you don't want to take a bath, then don't come.

74

"That should should bring them," Paul said. And it did. The Clintons appeared promptly at six on the big night.

The First Act:
Jerry and Nancy in *Pinocchio*

NANCY APPEARED ON A LITTLE STAGE in front of a curtain. She wore a long nose like Pinocchio's, but she had *shrunk* to only 2½ feet tall. Nobody in the audience could figure out how she had made herself so short. She sang a song she had made up and did a little tap dance. The song went something like this:

I know My nose
You know It grows
That my name Every time I tell
Is Pinocchio. A lie.

So here goes, I'm no good
I chose Made of wood
To speak now Would be good
Of my nose. If I could . . . . .

I've forgotten the rest of the lyrics, but you get the idea. It was something to see because all during the time she was singing, her tiny legs were dancing and when she sang a line like "would be good, if I could," both feet would come up off the stage and she'd hover there as if she had discovered a way to defy gravity. Both feet would be off the stage for a full five seconds or as long as she held a note.

It was a great act, and I could see the Clintons were very impressed. After it was over, Matthew Clinton stood up and clapped and shouted "Bravo" until Lard Clinton slapped his shoulder and slammed the little guy back into his chair.

After the show, when the Clintons had gone home, Nancy and Jerry told

JERRY'S HANDS ARE NANCY'S AND NANCY'S HANDS ARE NANCY'S FEET.

us how they did it. Pinocchio's arms were really Jerry's, while his legs and feet were really Nancy's arms and hands. Of course, no one could see Jerry during the act, because he was hidden behind a curtain.

The Second Act:
Paul and I in
A Night at the Flicks

PAUL HATED GETTING UP ON STAGE, and I had a hard time memorizing lines, so our act had to be pretty simple. We did a stunt I remembered from camp. First, you turn off all the lights, and the actors take their places in the dark. Then one kid turns on a flashlight, points it at the actors, and waves it back and forth. Simple, but it creates the effect of an old silent movie. Those old movies were called the "flickers." And that's exactly what you do with the flashlight. You flick its beam on and off the actor. Another effective technique is to hold the flashlight still in your left hand and block the light with your right hand. When you move your right hand up and down as fast as you can across the face of your flashlight, the illusion of an old silent movie is perfect. Keep your right hand about three inches in front of the flashlight. Relax your wrist so that it is limp. Keep your fingers closed.

Practice this in a dark room with a friend moving in front of you. It is your friend's *continued* motion broken by your right hand acting like a camera shutter that makes this trick work.

Somewhere I dug up an old plinkety-plonk piano recording. Just the right background music for an old Charlie Chaplin movie.

So I got dressed up like this.

We turned off the lights, put on the record, Paul started firing with his flashlight, jiggling it rapidly to and fro over my antic figure, and we were a smash.

Afterwards, young Matthew stood up and clapped and shouted "Bravo" until Lard pulled him down again.

MOVE YOUR HAND UP AND DOWN ACROSS THE FACE OF YOUR FLASHLIGHT,

I DO CHARLIE CHAPLIN.

OHHHHH, THE PAIN! OHHHH...

The Third Act:
The Clintons in
A Shadow Show

THE CLINTON BROTHERS HAD BROUGHT a sheet and some wire. When their turn came, they asked permission to take the paintings off two facing walls. I said, "Sure, that's okay." They then strung the wire between the hooks that had held the pictures. "Is this going to be a high wire act?" Jerry said wittily. He roared with laughter and slapped me on the back.

Paying no attention to Jerry, the Clinton Brothers went right on with their work, hanging a bed sheet from the wire with safety pins. Actually, their preparations were almost as interesting as the show that followed. With Mother's help, they got together a weird collection of things: a table, a saw, a lot of string, a drill, tires, and lots of other odd objects. We sat there for fifteen minutes waiting for them "to get their act together."

Finally, they asked that the lights be turned out. Young Matthew played a musical introduction on his harmonica that sounded like a bugle call for a cavalry charge. Then a light went on behind the sheet, and Scratch Clinton intoned "THE DOCTORS OPERATE." Scratch then did the horror movie laugh — "Hee, Hee — Haw, Haw, Ho — Ho, Ha Ha . . ."

Ebon and Lard Clinton were silhouetted behind the sheet, standing behind a table with Scratch laid out on it. The "doctors" pretended to saw away at the "patient's" stomach, then reached in and drew out lots of string. We all went "ohhhhhhh" except Nancy.

Nancy went "Eeeeek!"

After the string, Ebon and Lard pulled all sorts of things out of the patient — tin cans, tires, lawn mowers, stuff like that. Actually, it was a pretty good show, and the Clintons had as much fun doing it as we did watching it.

77

MATTHEW PLAYED RACHMANINOFF'S
PIANO CONCERTO IN C MINOR
ON HIS MOUTH ORGAN.

The best part of the night wasn't on the program at all. It was Matthew Clinton playing his harmonica.

He didn't stand up, let alone get up on stage. Sitting right in his seat, he played "Old Man River," "The Night the Frog Fell in the Well," and "Dixie." Finally, he gave us Rachmaninoff's "Concerto in C Minor," and we all clapped and shouted "Bravo."

Then we all trooped into the dining room, where Mother had laid out a mighty spread of cakes, doughnuts, and Whoopie Pies (they're called Suzy Q's these days). There was a bucket of ice on the floor stuffed with Coca-Cola, ginger ale, root beer, and one bottle of Moxie that Scratch and Lard fought over.

The prize for the best act was a small pocket flashlight with a key chain at-tached. Everyone agreed it should go to young Matthew. If we had given him a solid gold Oscar, he couldn't have been more pleased.

We ushered the Clintons to the door and stood watching them disappear into the night. We were just about to go back inside to clean up when from the snow-covered hill above the house we heard Matthew's harmonica one more time. He was playing "Taps."

Day is done
Gone the sun
From the lake
From the hill
From the sky,
All is well, safely rest
God is nigh. *

---

*The words to "Taps" are used courtesy of Widener University, Chester, Pennsylvania.

CHAPTER SEVEN
Spring Is on the Way . . .

Maple Syrup

IN THE NORTHEAST SECTION OF this country, after the snow and before the rain each spring, when days are bright and warmer, and nights still cold, a sweet water circulates up through the sugar maple. There is no solid evidence as to whether it is drawn up or pushed up. There is reason to believe, however, that sap flows downwards as well as upwards. When the sap is running and you tap a tree, you will be interrupting that flow and drawing off the sap in a container. It will not hurt the tree any more than it would hurt your house to draw from its plumbing a pail of water. That is, if you do it properly.

TAP A MAPLE

1. Make only one taphole in a tree if the tree is only 10 inches in diameter. If the tree is 20 inches in diameter then you may make two tapholes.
2. Drill the hole 3 inches deep into the tree, pitching the drill slightly upwards and using a ⅜-inch wood bit in your drill.
3. If you're drilling more than one hole in a giant maple, you may make as many as five or six tapholes.

Your local hardware store carries a line of sap spouts (also called "spiles").

Insert the spout into the taphole and seat it lightly with a hammer. By tapping the spout gently, you will be less apt to split the layer of inner bark.

Empty coffee cans with plastic tops make good sap buckets. With a hammer and nail, punch two holes near the top of the can, across from each other. Thread a piece of wire through the holes to serve as a "bail" handle for the bucket. Cut a triangle out of the plastic cover, replace the cover, and hang the bucket to the hook of your spout, so that the spout is over the hole in the plastic cover. You're in business.

While the sap is dripping into your buckets, make an Evaporator. Today's evaporators can be very complicated, but you can get by nicely with a simply constructed firebox.

Find a flat area of ground near your maple grove. Clear an area five feet by six feet of snow, sticks, and whatever. Place stones or cement blocks close together on the cleared area, building them up as shown.

Now you need a grill. If you can't find one large enough in your garage, six iron pipes would be fine, or use an old fire screen. Borrow a large kettle from your mother's kitchen.

BOILING SAP TO SYRUP

When you boil sap, you are removing its high water content through evaporation. Evaporation turns water into a gas or steam which dissipates into the air. What will be left when you're done will be maple syrup, which you can sell for big bucks per gallon. Sounds great, but remember that only five percent of a gallon of sap will remain as maple syrup when you're done boiling. When you consider the time and money involved in boiling sap, you can see why maple syrup costs so much in the store.

These instructions on how to boil sap could have been written a hundred years ago, but they still work fine.

Build a fire, light it, and wait until it is going strong. Place your kettle on the grill over the fire.

Pour in about four inches of sap and let it come to a boil. As the sap begins to thicken, add more sap. Keep the fire going strong and continue to boil.

You can add more sap again, if you wish, when the sap in the kettle begins to thicken — or, you can bring your current kettle of boiling sap to syrup now. Any thermometer registering up to 250 degrees Fahrenheit will show that the syrup is ready when it registers about 220 degrees Fahrenheit — or 8 to 12 degrees above the boiling point at your altitude.

If you don't have a thermometer, here are some very vague old-time directions. Take your pick.

1. Boil until the syrup is ready.
2. Boil the sap until about 95 percent of it has been evaporated.
3. Boil the sap for as long as it can boil and not burn.

PURE SAP... ...GETTING THERE...

To test boiling sap to see if it has become syrup, here's a foolproof way that's pretty simple. Find a utensil with a flat surface, such as a spatula or even a smooth shingle. Dip the utensil in the boiling sap or syrup, take it out, and see if the sap "aprons." If it is pure sap, it will drop off the spatula in small droplets as water would. But when it begins to scallop, your sap is approaching syrup. And when it finally "aprons," you have pure maple syrup.

...PURE SYRUP.

You must move fast now. Take the kettle off the fire. By the time the syrup cools, it may drip off your spatula in sheets the size of a silver dollar. Now, your syrup is ready to bottle and sell for big money. A gallon of good syrup will get you about twenty dollars.

Walk with a Staff

WALK ALONG – STEP OFF – AND SWING – EASY.

WALKING THROUGH THE WOODS, you're sure to encounter barbed-wire fences, stone walls, brooks, and streams. These obstacles can ruin a hike unless you carry a walking stick of some kind. A staff like Robin Hood's is a stout stick some six inches taller than you are. (Two or more of them are called "staves," according to *Webster's Dictionary.*)

You can use your staff simply as a walking stick, but you can also use it to pole vault over stones and puddles, and, as you practice, over fences and over brooks. You can also move very fast in the woods with it. Moreover, you don't have to be an Olympic track star to use it properly.

Just walk along, and now and then use your staff to lift your body a little. Use it like a super cane. Now, try it with both hands. Keep your hands above your head and swing your feet forward as you plant your staff. Try to swing up and over a log or ditch or large stone. You walk along, then set your staff. Step off and lift with your arms. Now swing real easy. Up and over. But don't try it first over a barbed-wire fence.

Paul, Jerry, Nancy, and I always had staves when we were walking in the woods. We'd have little contests to see who could get over whatever the neatest. They were just staves, but you know, when we got to high school we turned out to be very good at pole vaulting. (I even won the championship one year.)

Swinging Birches
— After Robert Frost

When I see birches bend to left and right
Across the lines of straighter darker trees,
*I like to think some boy's been swinging them.**

THE GREAT AMERICAN POET ROBERT Frost didn't make that up. *We* used to swing birches. Much later, when I was in college, I told a friend of mine from the city that as a boy I had done that.

"*You* can swing birches?" he asked.

We were camping on Mount Chocorua at the time. Nearby stood a birch tree that I told my friend I would swing, if he was really interested. He was.

I started up the tree. About halfway to the top I realized I couldn't remember the one key thing in swinging birches that *you must not do.* But I kept climbing, hoping that what I had forgotten would come to me along the way. When I was near the top and the birch had begun to bend under my weight, I reached out and grabbed a branch extending from its trunk. And the instant I swung out, I remembered *this* was what *you must not do.*

Too late.

The branch peeled off like a banana skin, ripping the white bark all along the trunk and I came down — down through thirty feet of branches, landing in disarray at my friend's shoes.

"Is that," he asked, "how one swings birches?"

"Well, sort of," I said.

DO **NOT** REACH OUT TO SWING THE BIRCH FROM AN EXTENDED LIMB.

HERE'S HOW YOU *SHOULD* SWING A BIRCH

Find a tree to suit your weight — one not too big, one not too weak. It should lean a little. Climb up it along the outside of its curve — not on the inside, or you'll bend it only halfway down before you have a chance to really swing it. Climb as high as you can. Near the top, the tree will start to bend. Grasp the trunk as high up as you can on the inside of the bend, hold on tight, and swing your body out and around under the bend. The tree will droop down under your weight. Most trees won't take you all the way to the ground. You'll probably have to drop the last two feet.

CAW CAW

CAW

SWING THE TRUNK.

..TO SWING A BIRCH PROPERLY, REACH OUT AND GRASP THE TRUNK.

SPRING IS A GOOD TIME TO MAKE STILTS

Find two two-by-fours six or seven feet long. The wood should be as free of knots as possible. Cut a shoulder into each of the two-by-fours 2 feet from the bottom, as shown. Now cut two blocks of two-by-four lumber and insert one into the shoulder of each stilt leg. You can use the piece you removed as a pattern for the slant of the blocks, so they will fit perfectly. Glue the blocks in place with white glue.

Now drill two holes ⅛ inch in diameter through the rear of the stilts and into the blocks. Drill each hole about 1½ inches deep.

Now, using ⅜-inch screws, screw each stilt leg to its block.

For added strength, a piece of one-inch board cut to the proper shape can be screwed on either side of the stilt leg and block. This will also increase the size of your foothold.

The top half of each stilt should be whittled round for a good hand grip. If you are working with pine, you can do this job with a sharp jackknife. Sandpaper the stilt handgrip smooth, and you're all set to start walking tall.

For mounting your stilts, you will have to find a fence you can use to steady yourself. After you've gotten handy with your stilts, you won't need a fence. You'll be able to hop right up on

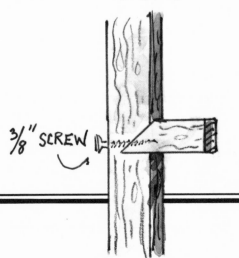

the foot blocks and walk off smartly.

The upper parts of the handles go behind your shoulders as shown. Your hands should hold the handgrips down at the level of your hips.

It'll take a little practice before you get the hang of it, so be patient with yourself.

STEADY, NOW...

CHAPTER EIGHT
A Spring Project

A Five-Foot Sailboat

IN APRIL OF THAT YEAR, THE HAWKS held a meeting to decide on a spring project to work on until school let out. That's when Paul told us that we ought to build a navy. He said we'd start by building a sailboat.

I thought he was losing his mind. None of us knew how to sail a sailboat, let alone build one. But Paul said we weren't going to build an America's Cup racer — just a simple sailboat. He had a book that told how it was done. The book didn't have any illustrations, but as he read it aloud to us, I drew up plans from what he was reading.

The first thing you have to do, the book told us, was to get your hands on some *seasoned,* or air-dried, lumber. The best lumber for a project like this would be white cedar. But pine works fine and is less expensive. The trick is to find boards that are free of knots. The nails have to be either copper or galvanized, or you could do a first-rate job and use brass screws. We decided on a second-rate job, with galvanized nails.

The sailboat's hull would be basically that of a five-foot *punt.* As you can see from the drawing, a punt doesn't come together at the bow the way a rowboat

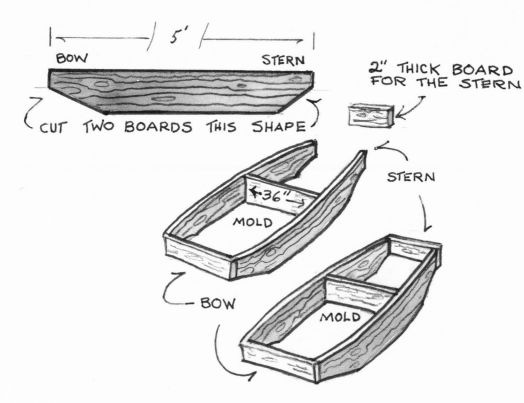

BOW STERN

5'

CUT TWO BOARDS THIS SHAPE

2" THICK BOARD FOR THE STERN SECTION

STERN

36"

MOLD

BOW

MOLD

does, so it's quite a lot easier to build.

Still it does have a shape. You'll notice the mold in the center is 36 inches wide, while the bow and the stern ends are both 30 inches wide. In the profile view, you can see that we planned to taper her hull, fore and aft (that's sailor's talk, you know).

We were ready to begin. Selecting two of the nicest knot-free pieces we could find, we sawed each to exactly five feet long.

We cut off the corners of the side boards as shown, then we took the boards to a farm pond, weighted them so they sank, and let them stay in the pond two days to soak so they'd bend easily around the mold.

Then we brought them back from the pond, good and soaked, and nailed each one to the bow piece. The mold in place, we bent the soaked side boards around the mold, nailed them to it, and pinched in the aft ends to nail to the stern piece.

The rest was easy (or so we thought!). We tipped the boat over and nailed on bottom boards cut from ¾-inch-thick lumber to the hull. The planks were nailed on close against each other but not jammed tight because the wood would swell when wet. We filled in the spaces between the planks with 1-inch quarter-round molding.

Next, we cut more ¾-inch boards for the forward deck, then turned the boat over again and nailed the deck boards across the sides and bow.

We had a tough time getting a mast and a boom for the boat, but Nancy's aunt, who ran a secondhand furniture store, finally came up with just what we needed — two 6-foot spruce dowels 1½ inches in diameter, one for the mast and one for the boom. Paul squared off the end of the mast with a hammer and chisel so it would fit into the bottom mast step.

We made the mast steps, or mast holders, from pieces of two-by-four. As

90

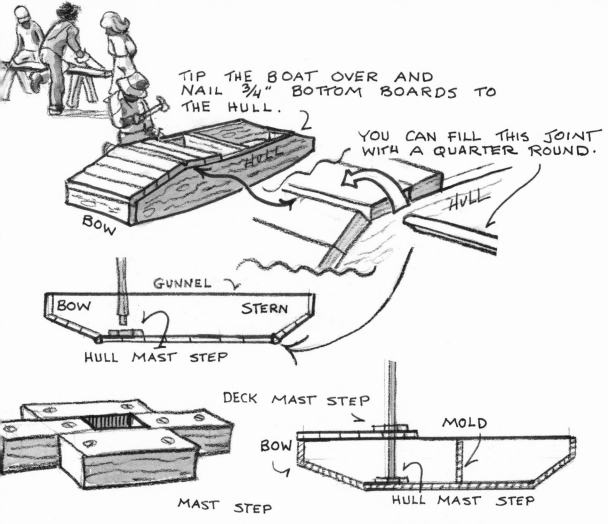

TIP THE BOAT OVER AND NAIL 3/4" BOTTOM BOARDS TO THE HULL.

HULL

BOW

YOU CAN FILL THIS JOINT WITH A QUARTER ROUND.

HULL

GUNNEL

BOW   STERN

HULL MAST STEP

DECK MAST STEP

MOLD

BOW

HULL MAST STEP

MAST STEP

you can see from the drawing, you need two mast steps, one for the floor of your hull and another for the deck. Screw the mast steps on with eight 2½-inch (long) screws.

Meanwhile, Nancy was making the sail. For a sail, you need strong, closely woven cloth. Burlap sacks are loosely woven and won't hold the wind. Canvas, of course, is best, but expensive. A sheet will do — or you can raid the family rag bag, as Nancy did, and patch a sail together from whatever closely woven bits of material you can find.

The hull was painted with red marine paint. Just regular paint won't do — you need *marine* paint. We put on three coats. The first coat was very thin, cut with turpentine. We allowed two days drying time between each coat. We didn't paint the inside.

Finally, for the rudder, Paul came up with a simple but ingenious idea. We drilled a hole in the aft board and fixed an oarlock there. (That's why he had used a board two inches thick for the stern section.) Then we found an old canoe paddle (gleaning again!), and that was the rudder.

"She's beautiful," Jerry said. "Where do we launch her?" Silence hung heavy on us. "I mean," said Jerry, persisting, "the nearest lake is ten miles away and Cobb's Farm Pond isn't big enough to take a bath in. Where do we launch her?"

"Never thought of that," said Paul. "I guess we'll have to build a lake."

"Avast!" said Nancy. (That's sailor's talk, too, you know; she thought it meant "Forward." We found out later that it meant "Stop!")

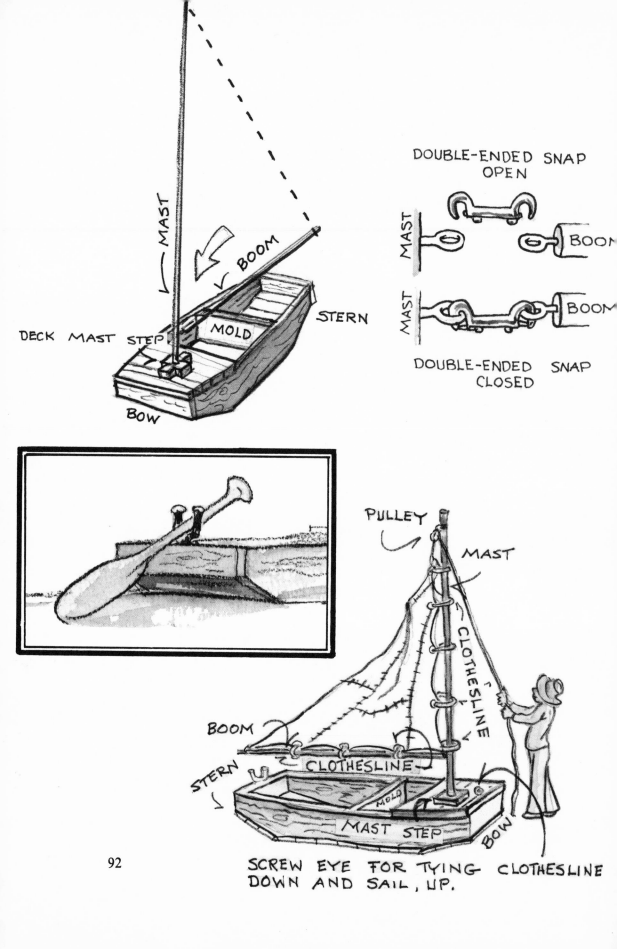

MAST

BOOM

DECK MAST STEP

MOLD

STERN

BOW

DOUBLE-ENDED SNAP
OPEN

MAST

BOOM

MAST

BOOM

DOUBLE-ENDED SNAP
CLOSED

PULLEY

MAST

CLOTHESLINE

BOOM

CLOTHESLINE

STERN

MOLD

MAST STEP

BOW

92

SCREW EYE FOR TYING CLOTHESLINE
DOWN AND SAIL, UP.

FAY FALLS

WE TOOK A WALK TO LOOK FOR A DAM SITE,

CAMERON CREEK

We Kill Two Birds with One Stone

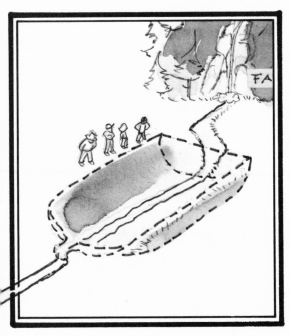

TO BUILD A LAKE, YOU NEED WATER and a dam. So the four of us took a walk along Cameron's Creek in Christian Hollow, looking for a dam site. The creek ran a crooked route from Fay Falls down through Cobb's 20-acre lot which everybody called Cobb's Field.

"What we're looking for," Paul told us, "is a shape in the land that looks like the bottom half of a bottle."

We found the perfect spot just about where we'd wanted to find it. Every now and then our group would "luck out" that way. "If we put the dam right here," Paul said, "we'll have a real pond." We figured that a dam four feet tall and six feet wide would create a body of water four times the size of a tennis court, large enough for our navy and deep enough to dive into.

93

A SHALLOW DIVE.

"That will require a shallow dive," said Jerry.

We decided to build an underground hut at the same time. Since our dam was going to be constructed of grain bags full of dirt, we had to get the dirt from someplace — why not get it all from just one place and use the hole left over for an underground hut? And not just your ordinary hut, but one *with an escape route*!

"Why do we need an escape route?" Nancy asked nervously.

"You never can tell when you'll need an escape route," I said. "It's always good to have one." Everybody nodded wisely as if they understood. That was nice, for I wasn't at all sure *I* understood.

Looking around, we found a site for our underground hut about two hundred feet away from where we thought the waterline of our man-made pond would come. The site was high and dry and would overlook the soon-to-be lake.

We placed eight stones to mark the shape of the hut on top of the ground, then cut the top layer of sod inside the stones (sod is the grass plus the three or four inches of topsoil directly beneath it) into one-foot squares for easy removal. We were careful not to hurt the grass any more than we had to and careful lifting out each square to keep it together. We piled the pieces of sod off to one side.

Once we had removed all the sod from the marked area, we could start digging in earnest. And we could start

PAUL CUTS OUT 1' SQUARES OF SOD. I START DIGGING...

WHILE NANCY AND JERRY PILE THE SQUARES OF SOD OUT OF THE WAY.

filling the grain bags with dirt for our dam. At first, Jerry and Paul did the digging, and I filled the grain bags. Nancy held the bags open for me. Nancy and I would fill each bag about three quarters full of dirt and wire the neck of the bag tight. Clothesline rope or even strong twine would have done just as well, but as we had wire, we used wire. Paul and Jerry kept digging, and Nancy and I kept sandbagging. We made another pile of the filled grain bags.

Then we switched off. Paul and I did the digging and Jerry and Nancy did the sandbagging. Nancy had found her specialty holding the grain bags open, but

Paul, Jerry, and I kept rotating our work. When we had enough bags full of dirt, I hitched up Spotlight to The Chariot, and we hauled the heavy bags down to the dam site.

We piled the filled grain bags into the bottleneck of the creek, laying them into position like the bricks in a brick wall. With all of us working together, we managed to complete the dam in four hours. By six that evening, the water was already beginning to rise behind it, and we decided to head home.

"While we wait for the water to fill," Paul said the next day, "let's finish up the underground hut."

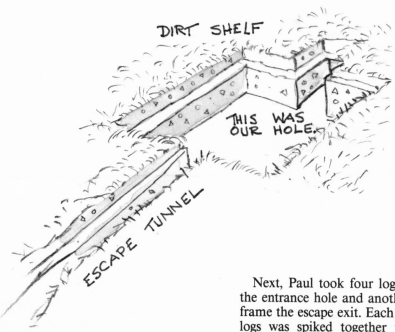

DIRT SHELF

THIS WAS OUR HOLE.

ESCAPE TUNNEL

By now, the hole for our underground hut looked like this. The rest was easy. We cut down saplings from the woods, trees about six inches in diameter. We trimmed off the branches and laid the poles across the top of the hole as close together as possible, resting the ends on the dirt shelf, then covered the poles with a good layer of dirt.

Next, Paul took four logs to frame the entrance hole and another four to frame the escape exit. Each set of four logs was spiked together to form a square frame. Before setting the frames into the ground, he measured them carefully. That night he built the hatch doors in his cellar at home. They were hinged and framed and had bolt locks on both the inside and the outside. Paul spiked the hatch doors to the entrance and escape-exit frames.

Finally, we covered the whole area with the sod we had cut out first, plac-

WE STARTED CHUCKING THE DIRT ON TOP OF THE LOGS.

NANCY CHECKED OUT THE ESCAPE TUNNEL

PAUL'S HATCH SYSTEM

SOD

DIRT

LOGS

ESCAPE TUNNEL

ing the squares neatly together over the hut roof to look like undisturbed grass. Very soon, when the sod grew back together, the roof *would* be grass!

The only thing we had left to do was to cut a hole in the roof of the underground hut so we could build a fire in it. That would be our chimney, and it was easy to do. Find a place in your roof where the roof poles don't fit too well together, where the dirt covering them wants to trickle down anyway, and scrape out the dirt. Make a hole to the outside world through the sod cover, and now you can build a fire in the hut — as long as you build it *directly* beneath the hole. But leave the hatches open for a draft for your fire and fresh air for your lungs. Keep your fire *very small* — just a "smudge."

LEAVE A HOLE IN YOUR ROOF AND YOU CAN BUILD A FIRE DOWN THERE.

COVER YOUR HATCHES WITH LEAVES AND SUCH.

97

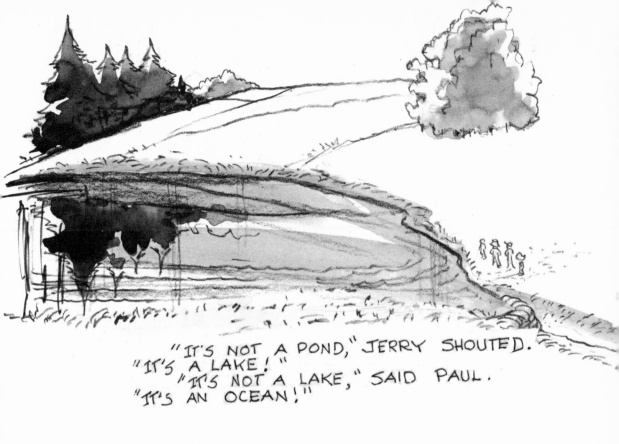

"IT'S NOT A POND," JERRY SHOUTED.
"IT'S A LAKE!"
"IT'S NOT A LAKE," SAID PAUL.
"IT'S AN OCEAN!"

When we were done with the hut, we walked down to our new dam to see if the water level had risen. It had. Indeed, that body of water looked more ocean than pond or even lake. It was certainly large enough for our sailboat. Time at last to launch her!

And when we did, she sank.

...AND WHEN WE LAUNCHED HER, THE FIRST THING SHE DID WAS SINK.

WE PRESSED ONE OR TWO STRANDS OF CANDLE WICKING IN EACH JOINT AND THEN APPLIED A THIN COAT OF PAINT.

We Caulk a Boat

"I EXPECTED SHE'D LEAK A BIT AT first — until the wood swelled," Paul said.

"Leak a *bit*?" I wondered. "Doesn't he realize the boat's on the bottom of the lake?"

Pushing and pulling and puffing, we hauled the boat's bow back on the bank — high enough up so we could bail her out. When we had enough water out of her so that she could float on her own, we dragged her entirely out of the water, removed her mast and boom, and rolled her over on her gunnels.

By noon the next day, she was dry, but while the wood had swelled some, and the seams were tighter, she'd probably still "leak a bit." We decided to caulk her. Laying one or two strands of candlewicking in each "joint," or seam, we rolled it in firmly and then we applied a thin coat of paint, working the paint into the seams as we went along. We let the paint dry for two days. Then we filled the seams with a commercial seam-filler or caulker.

Next day, when we launched her for the second time, we had Nancy christen her the *Nancy Belle*. Paul, Jerry, and I then slid her, aft end to, back down into the lake. She floated on the water, sitting up pert and dry like a proud duck. We all cheered, then replaced the mast and boom and rigged the sail. Paul had Nancy climb in and sit amidships. He climbed in after her and hoisted the sail. Off they went across Lake Hawk, sort of skittering sideways. It didn't look like they were in all that much control.

THEN NANCY BURST INTO TEARS.

Every time Paul tried to come about, she'd roll almost to her beam ends. I'd been reading a book on sailing so I knew terms like that, now. What it means is that every time Paul tried to turn the *Nancy Belle* around, she'd start to tip over. Finally, at the far end of the lake a gust of wind spanked her sail in mid-turn, and the *Nancy Belle* turned turtle. For the second time that week, we hauled her up out of the lake. Then all four of us collapsed on the ground, panting and giving the *Nancy Belle* dirty looks. Nancy even stuck her tongue out at her.

"Wouldn't you know," Nancy said, finally, "that anything that didn't work would be named after me."

"Ancient mariners believed that a woman on board a ship was bad luck,"

Jerry muttered. Nancy burst into tears. None of us boys knew what to do about that. Paul did slap Jerry on the shoulder with the back of his hand, but it didn't stop Nancy from crying.

All of a sudden, Paul leapt to his feet, shouting, "*I* know what's wrong with that boat! She doesn't have a *keel*!"

"What's a 'keel'?" said Jerry.

"Well, my brother has a canoe. He's rigged it for sailing and he has sort of underwater outriggers on it. He told me the outriggers were in place of a *keel*. I let it go at that because I didn't know what a keel was. Now Nancy and I just keeled over out there on the lake. *That's* what a keel is — to stop you from keeling over." Paul was exultant. That night he built an outrigger thing in his workshop.

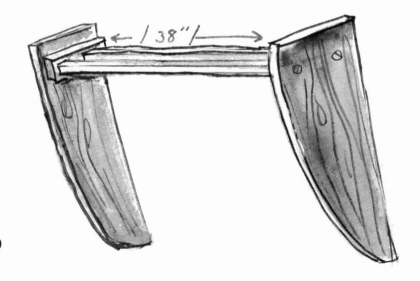

100

Success at Last

THE NEXT MORNING, WE ALL MET AT the lake. Aft end to, the *Nancy Belle* was slipped once more back into the lake. Once more, Nancy piled into the boat. Paul climbed in with a rig that looked like two giant rabbit ears held together, not by the head of a rabbit, but by two two-by-fours. He settled his outrigger on the gunnels. Both ears sliced down into the dark water like knives. With "C" clamps, he clamped the outrigger to the *Nancy Belle* on both sides. Up went the sail. It flapped lazily in the wind, until he turned the boat windward with his paddle. And then, the small sail snapped taut with a light and sudden crack. The *Nancy Belle* leaned away from it — but she didn't roll. She caught hold of the wind and raced across the lake.

Jerry and I roared with laughter — not because anything was funny — but because everything was working. We jumped up and down and pounded each other with our fists. At the far end of the lake Paul "came about," and back sped the *Nancy Belle*. And I could see even from the shore that the biggest and brightest thing about her was Nancy Galloway's smile. So the following day, when no one else was around, I painted her name on the stern board. Not knowing what *belle* meant — I painted a bell beneath the letters.

A Hillside Bunker

AS WE HAD ABOUT TWENTY EMPTY grain bags left over from building the dam, we decided to build a hillside bunker into Black Jack's Bluff. (Permanent bunkers in World War Two were made of concrete and reinforced with steel. But some battle lines were not planned to be permanent, and the bunkers positioned along those lines were made of logs and dirt and dirt-filled sandbags.) It wasn't half as much work as the underground hut, but the technique was about the same.

First we cut out sections of sod. Setting them aside, we laid into serious digging. We filled the grain bags as before, wiring them tight.

Into the cavity dug in the bluff, an entrance frame was inserted, made from tree branches cut and trimmed. The pole roof was more trimmed branches resting on the dirt shelf. Again, we covered the poles over with dirt and fitted the sod squares together on top of the dirt. Lastly we built the front protection wall of dirt-filled bags.

102

END POST   DIRT SHELF.

END POST

SANDBAGS

JERRY WITH HIS DAISEY AIR RIFLE
DURING DEER SEASON; LOTS OF LUCK, JERRY.

BLACK JACK'S BLUFF.

CHAPTER NINE
Woodsmanship

THE RIVER

Don't Get Lost

SCHOOL LETS OUT IN EARLY JUNE IN New Hampshire. Summer doesn't really come until July, and August is the hottest, laziest month of the year. But June is welcome. The air is clear, the nights still cool, and the sun fairly dances over the land. We spent a lot of time in the woods.

We'd take walks covering as much as fourteen miles in a single day. We'd get lost, now and then, but not *very* lost. All we'd have to do was climb a tree and locate the Connecticut River, which is west of Walpole on the map and which we knew ran north and south. This gave us three points of the compass which is two more points than you really need.

Nevertheless, it is true that you really do wander in circles when you're lost in the woods. For a time it's curious, but after a while, it's terrifying. The trick is to walk a *straight line* in any direction — if you can do this, sooner or later you'll hit a road, a house, or a village. If you don't recognize where you are, you can always ask somebody. But if you're out in the bush walking in circles, you may be out in the bush walking in circles forever.

A compass is your best bet to help keep you going in a straight line. But if you don't happen to have one handy, you can use your watch. It's a neat trick. Here's how you do it.

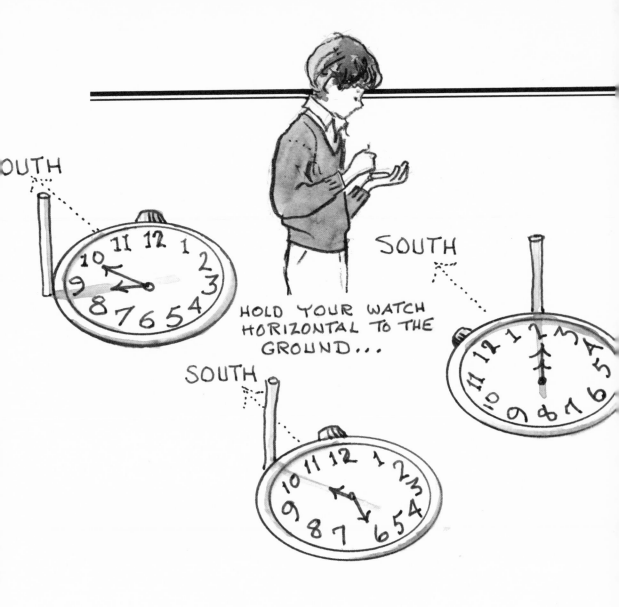

SOUTH

SOUTH

HOLD YOUR WATCH
HORIZONTAL TO THE
GROUND...

SOUTH

A WATCH CAN WORK AS A COMPASS

The next time you're lost in the woods on a sunny day, use your wrist watch as a compass. Hold your watch horizontal to the ground, face up in the palm of your hand. We'll suppose it is 8:50 a.m. Take a match or a very slim, straight twig, and hold this stick up-

right next to the rim of your watch at that place that the hour hand points to.

Now, turn slowly until the shadow of that stick aligns with the hour hand. When the shadow falls directly over the hour hand, the hour hand points to the spot on the horizon that is directly underneath the sun. South will then be exactly midway (halfway) between the hour hand and the number 12 on the face of your watch.

Now, let's try it again at 10:30 a.m. Using the same procedure, hold the stick upright next to the rim of your watch at the spot where the hour hand is pointing. Turn slowly until the shadow of the stick falls along the hour hand. Again, South will be halfway between the hour hand and the number 12 on the face of your watch. Since the hour hand of your watch points to 8 minutes before 12, South is therefore off the point of 4 minutes before 12.

In the p.m., the same rule of shadow holds, except that in the afternoon, the direction of South will be backward on the face of time. I'll explain. Let's say it's 2:10 p.m. in the afternoon. Turn the watch until the shadow falls along the hour hand that's pointing to the number 2 on your watch. Now, South is off the number 1 on your watch, still midway between 12 and the shadow, but on the other side of the watch face.

Practice this trick with your watch and check your success against a real compass. Do it at various times of the day to make sure you've got it just right.

There are two rather serious problems we must consider in this exercise: one, your watch should be going, and two, you can't do this at midnight. I have that on very good authority.

A QUICK STORM SHELTER

Use your hatchet or ax to cut from a tree branches about five feet long, straight, with one end forked, as shown.

Now interlock the forked ends and spread the pole bottoms so that you have a structure like a tepee.

Cut more straight poles a little taller than the first ones, without forks. Lay them closely together against the uprights on three sides. Leave an opening, planned to face away from the wind.

Next cut pine boughs and/or brush and pile closely together against the sticks. Now jump inside. You barely made it!

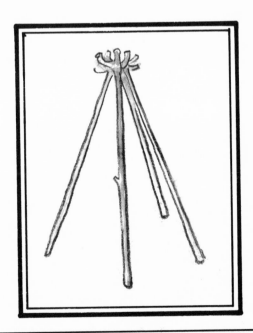

Camping Out

MOST OF THE TIME, WE'D COME home for dinner. But sometimes we'd eat lunch in the woods, and sometimes we'd camp out for the night. Lunch could be just sandwiches we had brought along, but occasionally we'd cook fish we'd caught, or hot dogs, or whatever over a camp fire. Then, too, we might decide to take a long hike out where we'd have to spend the night and bring more stuff. We'd talk or tell ghost stories over the dying embers of the fire. The thing about ghost stories is that the last one to tell a good ghost story is hoping to be the only person to get to sleep that night. I got it down to a fine art . . .

But first — the camp fire.

HOW TO BUILD A CAMP FIRE

In this activity, rule one is Safety First! Here is a short checklist to follow.

1. *Don't* build a campfire without first checking with your local fire department or game warden. Or ask your parents to check, and tell them where you'll be. There are times of the year when all growth is like tinder or paper, and you could end up with a Forest Fire.

2. *Don't* build a fire against a tree — dead or alive. If the tree is alive, your fire could kill it. If the tree is dead, it will burn as easily as your firewood.

3. Choose your fireplace area and clear the ground of twigs and brush.

4. Collect three or four flat stones and place them close beside each other, as a base for the fire, on the area you have cleared. If you borrow these stones from a stone wall, return them when you're done with your fire.

5. Check the direction of the wind, then pile stones around three sides of the fireplace base, as shown. To check the wind direction, lick your finger until it is wet, then hold it up and wait a few minutes; the dryest spot on your finger is the direction from which the wind is coming.

6. Time to collect wood. At first, think small. I always had great

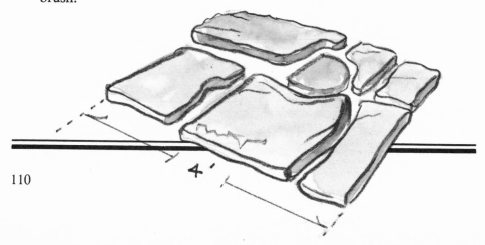

4'

32"

WIND DIRECTION

PAUL LICKS HIS
FINGER AND
TESTS FOR
WIND DIRECTION

luck collecting the dead twigs at the base of pine trees. They were easy to reach, there were plenty of them, and unless it was raining hard, they were always dry.

7. Look around for a dead tree or dead limbs. A branch two inches in diameter can be broken across your knee. You'll need a bunch of such two-inch sticks.

8. For larger pieces of wood, you'll need an ax or hatchet. If you're lazy, as I am, make sure the blade is sharp. A dull ax is good for nothing but smashing pumpkins. If you're into splitting wood, then make sure you split the wood *on* wood. Otherwise, you can blunt your hatchet or ax blade in the earth or on a stone.

9. Now you have three kinds of dry wood: twigs, sticks about two inches around, and small logs (split if you wish).

10. Time to build the fire. If you do this correctly, it will be a small, safely contained fire with concentrated heat. *Don't* build a bonfire; such a fire is hard to control and *very* dangerous. A good cooking fire is *small.*

11. If you forgot to bring paper, check your pockets for facial tissue, old scraps of paper, torn movie tickets, anything. A dollar bill will do just fine (that is, if you have money to burn). The tiny twigs you have collected mean that you need only just enough paper to start the twigs burning.

12. Crumple up the paper and

stack twigs around it like a te-pee. Have a pal standing by to pass you more twigs as you need them. Sometimes in the rainy season getting a fire going is as difficult as open-heart surgery, so you may need help.

13. Now then, I hope somebody remembered to bring matches. If so, you're in business. Strike a match and fire the paper. Now, watch it like a hawk. Blow on it, tenderly. Have someone pass you more twigs. Concentrate.

14. Now you have a blaze! A small blaze, understand, but a blaze. Your helper will start handing you the two-inch sticks. Stack these against each other, tepee-style again, and everything in your fireplace will start snapping, crackling, and popping.

15. Put a couple of small logs on when the kindling is glowing.

I'M BREAKING WOOD OVER MY KNEE. PAUL IS FANNING THE FIRE WITH HIS HAT. JERRY FEEDS THE FLAME WITH DRY TWIGS WHILE NANCY FINDS THE WOOD WE NEED.

COOKING OVER AN OPEN FIRE

POTATOES take the longest, so put them on the fire as soon as you have a nice glowing bed of coals below the new wood you put on top from time to time. Wrap unpeeled potatoes in aluminum foil (or roll them in mud) and place them right in the glowing coals. Turn them from time to time so that they will cook evenly. With a good fire, potatoes will bake in *about* an hour and a half.

MEAT. We used to bring steak from home, which we'd cut up into pieces and cook on a "spit" over the fire. Cube steak is fine — it's cheaper and cooks faster than real steak. Chunks of lamb or beef stew meat work well, too. To make a spit, cut from a sapling or young tree two straight, slender green branches, each with a two-pronged fork at one end. Sharpen the unforked ends with a knife or hatchet, and drive the sharpened ends into the ground on each side of your fireplace. Now cut another straight green stick long enough to reach between and extend beyond the two forked saplings planted upright in the ground. Whittle one end of this spit

stick so that is sharp, like a pencil point. Thread your chunks of meat (and bits of tomato and onion, too, if you have them) along this spit like a shish kebab, as shown. Rest the spit or skewer on the two forks of the two uprights, and turn the meat slowly over the fire. If someone remembered to bring butter, you can melt a little and dribble it over the meat as you turn the spit.

CORN ON THE COB. While one of you is making the meat rack, another can take care of the corn. Peel back the husks just enough so you can remove the cornsilk. Replace the husks around each ear, and soak the unhusked corn in a bucket of water (or the brook) until it is wet through — a matter of ten-fifteen minutes. While the ears soak, check your fire and add more wood if necessary. Keep it going well. Then place the soaked ears, still in their husks, around the edge of the fire. Turn them often to make sure they won't be raw on one side and burned to a crisp on the other. The corn should take about fifteen minutes to cook.

HOW TO START A GREAT GHOST STORY

Just the thing for an overnight camping trip. Your tents have been set up for the night, you've eaten well, and your campfire is beginning to die down. Maybe your group is becoming a little bit sleepy, a little bit bored. Time to wake them up with a first-rate ghost story.

The most important thing about a ghost story is mood. Mood is, somehow, wrapped up with setting and your introduction and your willingness to believe in the stuff you're using.

The purpose of a good ghost story is to scare everybody half out of their wits. DON'T say, "Hey gang, do you want to hear a first-rate ghost story?" because they will all say "No!" Instead, get their attention by saying, very seriously, very somberly — "Did I hear thunder?"

"I don't think so," somebody will respond. "Why?"

You've got their attention. "Because we're camping out on Satan's Hill," you say with some irritation.

"So?" somebody will ask.

"Well, we're camping out on *Satan's Hill*." Say these lines with fear. "There was a witch hung on this hill."

HERE'S HOW YOU KNIT YOUR EYEBROWS.

WHAT'S THAT?

"So?" the same somebody will ask.

Now then, back off. Say something like this. "This is neither the time nor the place to talk of such things . . . ."

Brood a bit. Look down at your hands, knit your eyebrows.

"Anyway," you say impatiently, "thunder is thunder, right guys?"

Toss it off with a laugh and look down at the fire again. Knit your eyebrows . . . .

"Are you suggesting that if we hear thunder, the witch hung here on Satan's Hill will return?" someone with imagination will surely ask you.

And then you whisper with passion. "What's *that?*" You should then look suddenly off in the direction of the woods.

"What's what?" they'll say in unison, if you've done it right.

"That!" you whisper, pointing into the dark woods.

What you're doing here is making them a part of a story they truly want to be a part of — and truly *don't* want to be part of.

At least, you still have their attention, and to that degree you are entertaining them. Now, press ahead by backing off again.

Say something like this. Sound brave. "I'm sorry, don't mind me." Knit your brows again. Look down at your hands, which should tremble just a bit. The fire is now a soft glow of ash. If you're lucky, there will be a roll of thunder from the west at this moment. A strong breeze out of the northwest will stir the branches above their heads.

"Was a witch *really* hung on this hill?" one of your friends will ask.

"On this hill?" Now go into a rage. "On this *hill?*" Jump to your feet, lift your arms above the fire, and shout . . . . "ON THIS VERY SPOT."

If you're very, very lucky, lightning will crack, thunder will roll, and you'll never have to finish the story. Your audience will head for cover, fast.

Put Out The Fire

If your evening hadn't ended with a good introduction to a ghost story and a drenching thunderstorm, it would have been your responsibility to put out the fire.

You can either drench it with water or smother it with dirt. In either case, you must quench the fire completely if there is no one there to watch it through the night.

TWO GREAT SLINGSHOTS

There is something fascinating about marksmanship. That is, sending forth a stone, an arrow, a bullet and hitting something. The pleasure has nothing to do with hunting or killing or destroying property. Just in itself, marksmanship is good fun, and a great way to while away the time with a friend on a long summer afternoon — particularly if you each have your own handmade slingshot. You will then be testing your craftsmanship as well as your marksmanship.

If you're in luck, your competition will have constructed the standard All-American Slingshot. Here's how to do that.

Start by cutting a green crotched (forked) stick from a tree. Notch it as shown. Cut two heavy (¾-inch-wide) elastic bands in half and tie an end of each around a notch in the fork. Cut an oblong piece of leather or canvas about three inches long by two inches wide. Cut a slit in each end, and thread the elastic band on each side through the slit. Then turn the band end back on itself, binding it by wrapping tightly with fishing twine. Tie the twine securely. (You can finish off with a knot rather than the twine wrap, but wrapping the ends makes a neater looking slingshot.)

Eighty years ago, every kid in town had one of these in his back pocket. Still, there is a better slingshot. It's very much like the standard one, but it is stronger, shoots farther, and is more accurate. However, you need big muscles to fire it!

Use a thicker, *stronger* crotched stick, and *two* rubber bands (or strips cut from an old inner tube) on each side, tied so as to leave only about three inches of rubber band on each side open to spring a walnut. Except for this important difference, you build it the same as the standard slingshot.

116

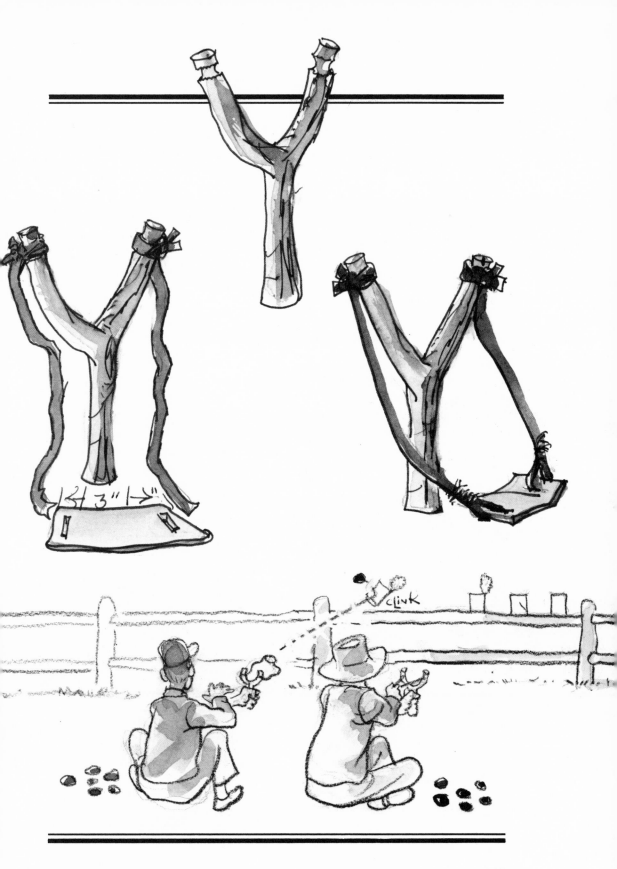

CLINK

CHAPTER TEN
The Great Apple Fight at Cameron Creek

READ THIS AS A GUIDELINE FOR AVOIDing battles. If you take over common ground, as we did, start calling it "ours," as we did, make the property interesting, and design a flag which you run up a flagpole and salute as we did — you could be asking for *War.* (That's how the American Revolutionary War started.)

It was October of the year 1942. Sunny days that were still warm gave way to sharp cold nights that hinted of winter. Early one evening Paul and I were holed up in the Hawks' underground hut. It was chilly, so we had a small fire of applewood going.

Jerry arrived and slid down into the hole, breathing fast, as though he'd run all the way from his house.

"They're coming!" he panted.

"Who's coming?" Paul asked.

"The Clinton Brothers," Jerry said.

"When?" said Paul.

"On Saturday. Two days from now. They're coming and there is going to be an apple war."

"An apple war?" I asked.

"Yes," said Jerry. "They've got two whole bushels of apples to chuck at us."

"Rotten apples?" Paul asked.

"Yes," said Jerry, "soft, smelly, rotten apples."

"Then we must make plans," Paul said. "We'll need a map of our territory for a strategy meeting on Friday night. Tomorrow we'll collect *four* bushels of crab apples."

"Crab apples?" I protested. "*They're* going to be throwing big, rotten apples. And *we're* going to be throwing little, tiny, crab apples?"

"No. We're going to be slingshotting little, tiny, HARD crab apples." Paul went on, "And we'll need armor for our faces and our bodies. I'm all set. My brother used to be catcher on the baseball team in Junior High. I'll use his face mask and body protector and his catcher's mitt as a shield. But you guys will have to work up your own armor."

"What about Nancy?" I asked. "Is she to be part of this?"

"No," said Paul. "Her mother would hang me upside down by my heels if she got hurt."

"Well then," I concluded, "we're go-

119

ing to have to be very good. There are four Clintons and only the three of us."

"That's right. But here's the worst of it. If the Clinton brothers can't do anything else, they sure know how to chuck a rotten apple."

Even while we were talking about our plans for the defense of our property, the Clinton Brothers were having their own meeting in the pig pen in their barn.

They had drawn their own map as well, which looked like this (see right). And while their map was brief, it did, at least, indicate North correctly.

Our map, which I am proud to say *I* drew, is shown bottom right.

I had to pace everything off in order to get the distances right. If I took very long steps from point to point, my stride covered 2 feet. If I took 20 paces, that meant I had covered 40 feet of ground. I used a compass always and made ten sketches placing things like our tree house and lookout tower, and

when it was all done, I worked out the general scale of my drawing by measuring a very sure distance on the map — 1 inch. If the distance between any two points was 500 feet, the distance on my map was 1 inch.

On Thursday, Paul, Jerry, and I worked from four o'clock (after school) until eight o'clock that night collecting four bushels of crab apples. I don't know about Paul, but Jerry and I faced angry parents when we finally got home. The worst of it was that we couldn't tell our parents why we'd been late. We couldn't tell our parents that we were in for trouble and facing War. That just isn't the kind of thing you *can* tell parents. I went to bed that night without supper because I was late for it.

The following evening, Paul, Jerry, and I met at the tree fort. I was even late for that, so I rode Spotlight to the meeting, full bent for leather. I brought my map, drawn on parchment, which is a nice touch as parchment paper has a

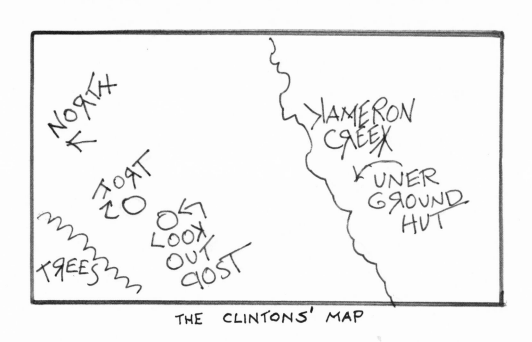

THE CLINTONS' MAP

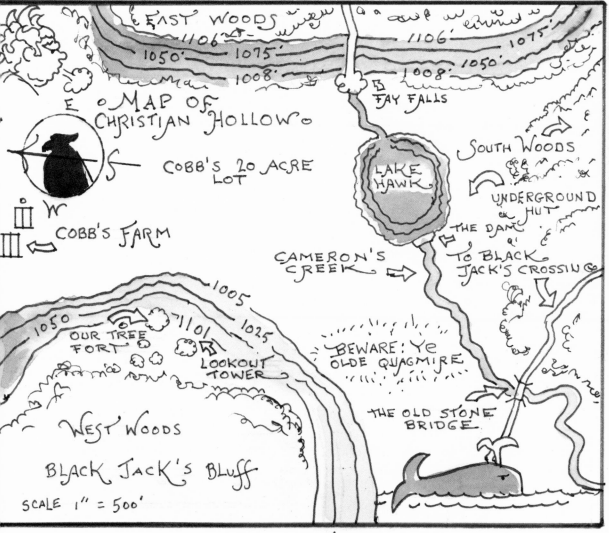

THE HAWKS' MAP

I RODE SPOTLIGHT FULL OUT TO GET TO THE MEETING.

SO, WE HAD A STRATEGY MEETING IN THE TREE FORT HUT.

certain rattle to it. I spread it out in front of us, under the lantern. "Say, now," said Paul, "that looks pretty good."

He tacked the map up on the wall so he could point to places on it with a stick. "My guess is they'll try to surprise us. They don't know that we know they're coming."

"But, we don't know they don't know that we know they're coming — do we?" I asked.

"I don't know," said Jerry.

"Well, even if they do know," said Paul, "that we know they're coming, they will still want to surprise us. My guess is they'll try to approach us from behind — from the west. There are heavy woods in that sector that will make good cover for them."

"Sector?" I asked.

"Yes, that's soldier talk." Paul went on, "We'll have two men on the lookout tower. That way, it will look like we plan to stand our ground there. You two will volunteer for that post. You'll have ammunition, a full bushel of apples, but no weapons, no slingshots. You'll just throw the crab apples."

"But I thought the whole point of crab apples was that we could slingshoot them," I objected.

"Slingshots are accurate, and they're great for range, but what's needed at the start here is wild fire power," explained General Paul. "If you both pick up three crab apples at a time and chuck them as fast as you can, they'll think we're panicking and lie low until we've used up all our ammunition."

"And what are you going to be doing? Listening to 'Little Orphan Annie'?" I asked.

There was an awkward silence. Paul just studied me. I shifted my weight from the left foot to the right foot and put my hands in my pockets. Then I pretended to observe the map with keen interest. The silence went on so long, I thought I had grown deaf or something. Paul studied the map again.

Finally, he said, "I will be up in the tall birch to their left. I'll be there with a carefully selected bag of the hardest apples in our arsenal."

"Arsenal?" Jerry asked.

"Yes," said Paul. "That's soldier talk. I will have a strong, accurate slingshot and easy targets. While you guys are making our counterattack *look* good, I'll be making it *feel* bad."

"I see," said Jerry. "Our wild counterattack will keep them down — so you'll have still targets to shoot at."

"Roger," said Paul. "We won't be able to hold that position for long. So you two will both have to take the Tarzan swing from the lookout tower to the tree fort together."

"How will you get to the tree fort?" Jerry asked.

"I'll swing the birch. It's pitched just right. When all three of us are there, we'll have two bushels of crab apples, two different kinds of slingshots and, of course, the protection of the fort. *We'll* have cover and *they* won't." Paul paused. "What do you think?" he said, just a shade anxiously.

"How are you going to swing a birch in your brother's body protector?" Jerry asked.

There was another taut silence. But this time, I had the feeling Paul was truly considering the question.

"We won't put on our armor until we get to the fort," he decided, framing each word slowly.

In the lantern over our heads, the candle had all but burned out. It was guttering and sputtering, drowning in its own wax. Paul blew it out, lit another candle, and stuck it in a bottle head. "It's my hope by the time we've unloaded *our* three bushels of apples on them, they will have spent *their* two bushels of apples on us. Maybe then they'll go home."

"I wouldn't count on that," I said.

Another dreadful silence. Jerry checked his fingernails, I focused on a knot in one of the floorboards, while

Paul scowled at me.

"Really," said Paul. "Why?" He made both words sound like bad language.

"Well, I mean, there are going to be crab apples all over the place — the ones *we* throw, and my guess is they'll start chucking our own ammunition right back at us. You have to understand the Clintons; for all their faults, they persevere.

"Persevere?" said Paul.

"Yes, that's psychology talk."

Paul laughed. "Go on."

"Well, the more those guys hurt, the harder they fight," I said.

"You make them sound like good guys."

"They're not all bad." I decided I had said enough. Outside, it had started to rain, indeed, it was pouring — sheets of water slashing down against our window and skylight. The wind howled and rocked the branches supporting our fort, stirring the floor beneath us.

"Well, suppose they don't go home," Paul said thoughtfully. "Then we slide down the pole and make for the bunker. We'll keep another bushel of apples there. That'll be our last stand."

"Do you think we're going to win this?" Jerry asked.

"I don't know," said Paul.

It was time to go home.

In the morning I was awakened by the cawing of crows. "The crow," I thought, as I lay between sleep and activity, "is like the raven and the vulture. A death symbol." On this particular day, I could have risen from my bed bravely to fife-and-drum music or even settled for bagpipes — anything but crows.

I plunged into the closet after my armor, one small cardboard box with holes cut in it for my eyes, and a bigger box with armholes. Once armored, I felt better. I was invisible. No, wrong word — *invincible.*

Spotlight and I took the shortcut through Taggert Lane. Paul and Jerry were already at the fort, hauling baskets of apples up into the tree with a pulley rope. Paul had divided the two fort bushels into three baskets so we'd each have our own supply of ammunition. Two other baskets had been placed on the lookout tower.

The remaining apples were in a grain bag. "Take that bag down to the bunker, Austin," Paul directed. "Empty it out on the floor there in three equal piles about two feet apart." I took off my armor and left it at the foot of the tree with Paul's stuff. Picking up the bag, I scrambled down the bank to the bunker to carry out my orders. It was dark and cool inside the bunker. By the

WE WENT HOME IN THE STORM.

SPOTLIGHT AND I
TOOK A SHORTCUT.

time I got back to the ridge, we were pretty near ready. The slingshots were lying on the fort deck.

We hauled up the armor and stuck it in the hut. Jerry had brought three jelly doughnuts and a canteen of water for breakfast, which we ate sitting on the fort deck. Paul, I could tell, was edgy. He wanted to get us to our posts; no telling when the enemy would appear. So we wolfed down the doughnuts, swigged a few swallows of water, wiped our mouths with our shirt sleeves, and descended the ladder.

"Take that ladder out of here," Paul directed, "and hide it. Do either of you know that blackberry patch near the elm — northwest of here?" We nodded. "Good," he said, "slide it in there and see that it is well hidden. Then there's just one more thing to do," Paul went on.

"What's that?" I asked.

"Run up the Hawk flag."

"The flagpole came down in last night's storm," Jerry said. "Didn't either of you notice?"

"Well, then I'll put it back up," said Paul impatiently. But when Jerry and I returned, he seemed to be having some trouble, so we gave him a hand.

Hand over hand, Jerry and I climbed the knotted rope to the lookout tower. Once on the platform, we hauled up the rope after us.

JERRY AND I HELPED PAUL
PUT UP OUR FLAG.

JERRY AND I KEPT A SHARP VIGIL.

Paul climbed up the birch with a bag of specially selected hard apples tied to his belt. Gripping his favorite and most deadly slingshot in his teeth, he looked like the pirate coxswain in *Treasure Island* going after young Jim Hawkins.

All we had to do now was wait. Digging out my one-dollar pocket watch, I checked the time — 9:15. It was a sunny day. Red and gold leaves lay beneath us like a patchwork quilt upon the ground. Above us, the sky was royal blue. The Hawk flag fluttered and snapped in the light breeze from the north.

Jerry and I stretched out on our stomachs, facing west, our hands knotted into fists, holding our chins up. It was so peaceful I fell off to sleep. Maybe Jerry did, too. In any case we were rudely awakened by Paul shouting urgently,

"THEY'RE COMING! They're coming from the EAST, not the West, RIGHT across the field! They're ID-IOTS! THEY'RE COMING! GET TO THE FORT. FAST."

Jerry and I scrambled to our feet. Paul climbed higher in his birch tree and swung to the fort. "THEY'RE COMING!" he shouted. "THEY'RE COMING!"

We untied the rope swing, took hold, and jumped off the platform of the lookout tower. We landed, rolling and tumbling, on the fort deck. It's one thing to start off with two guys on a rope swing, but it's impossible to land well, unless you're Tarzan and Jane.

"THEY'RE COMING!" Paul shouted again. I was beginning to believe him.

He pointed to the field below us. In-

126

PAUL SWINGS THE BIRCH
TO THE TREE FORT DECK.

127

deed, they *were* coming and with more style than I would have given them credit to plan for or to execute. They were marching in lockstep in a block of four with the little pig they called Uncle Thaddeus bringing up the rear, bobbing along behind them like a dinghy after a sailboat.

Ebon Clinton was carrying a flag. It was blood red with white letters that spelled "KIL." Just because they couldn't *spell* "Kill" didn't mean they *couldn't* KILL.

EBON STABBED HIS FLAGPOLE INTO THE ROOF OF OUR BUNKER.

♪♪ ♪ ... THE COMING OF THE LORD, ... CHING ON ...♪♪ ... ♪ ♪♪

Beside Ebon marched Scratch with Lard behind him. Taking giant steps to keep up, young Matthew was playing the "Battle Hymn of the Republic" on his harmonica. With empty gunny sacks slung from their shoulders, they came, marching and singing, "Mine eyes have seen the glory of the coming of the Lord . . ."

"That's strange," said Paul.

"What?" I asked.

"Where are their *apples*?" he said. "Where are the two bushels of rotten apples?"

"I don't know," said Jerry.

"All right, men, let's get into our armor."

I put on my body box and settled the helmet box over my head, so that I looked like something you'd see stacked in a warehouse.

Jerry's outfit was his father's old football helmet — with goggles. He put on his father's shoulder pads as well, and then he strapped on hockey shin pads to the calves of his legs. Somehow, each new piece added to his armor made him look smaller. We were ready.

The Clintons were now scrambling up the embankment below us. Our accurate slings were loaded and stretched for action.

"Hold your fire," Paul said. "They're not in range yet."

"Don't fire until you see the whites of their eyes," Jerry whispered. Matthew's music had stopped. There was an ominous silence now. We watched them clamber up the hill to the bunker. There they stopped, and Ebon stabbed his flagpole down through the roof. Scratch climbed into the bunker and started handing out the apples I had carefully stacked on the floor to his brothers, who loaded them into their empty gunny sacks.

"Look at that!" said Paul. "Without throwing a single apple, they have bypassed our lookout tower and taken over our bunker: our retreat position. And now they're taking our apples! For a dumb bunch, they're pretty smart."

Outraged, Paul let fly with his first shot. Ebon yowled as it caught his shoulder. It was a good shot, but then we did have the advantage of being up and shooting down.

"Let's try not to hit Matthew," Jerry said as he fired a shot at Ebon. He missed, but not by much.

They were coming on up the hill, now, and the closer they came the easier targets they became.

"HOLD YOUR FIRE," PAUL SAID. "THEY'RE STILL NOT IN RANGE."

We kept up a steady fire. There was always an apple in the air. I lost track of who hit whom. We definitely had the edge. The Clintons hadn't thrown a single apple. We had to be hurting them bad. Too good to last. Not twenty feet below the ridge, they halted and began to return our fire with purpose. Now apples began coming faster at us than we could answer. After all, the Clintons didn't have to load, aim, pull back, and let fire. They just threw.

My helmet was knocked off by a direct hit, but I let it lie. Jerry shed his shoulder pads, which interfered with his aim. Paul had taken off his face mask and body guard and was now using his baseball glove to catch apples in the air and chuck them right back where they came from. We still had the advantage of position — firing downhill and shielded by the fort.

"Don't go Paul's route," I thought.

"Take careful aim and hit the target. Don't answer shot for shot — just get them good."

And that's when I caught a rotten apple on the back of my head. "Somebody is coming up from behind," I shouted to Paul as I wriggled out of my body box.

"Hit the deck," Paul said. We all dropped flat on the platform, lying there face down, hands over our heads. Rotten apples were raining in from the west, crab apples from the east.

"I've figured it out," said Paul to the deck floor.

"You've figured what out?" said Jerry, in a muffled voice.

"Last night, after we left in the rain storm, the Clintons came here and looked over our situation. That is, they knew we knew they were coming. They knew we'd load the bunker with apples."

I CAUGHT AN APPLE ON THE **BACK** OF MY HEAD...

"You think they knew?" I asked.

"They brought their two bushels of apples up here somewhere and hid them on the ridge. They knew they couldn't carry them up the embankment to the ridge." A sudden barrage of apple splats shook the sides of the fort. We ducked again.

"*Who* is behind us?" I sort of scream-whispered. "*Who* found the Clintons' rotten apples? Who's chucking them at us?"

"*I* think it's the Rat River Bunch," said Paul.

"Oh no!" said Jerry. "The Rat River Bunch are much too old for this kind of thing. I thought by now they'd all been drafted."

"Well," said Paul, "They weren't. Instead, they found the Clintons' ammunition — two whole bushels of rotten apples — and they are at war with both the Hawks and the Clintons." To illustrate his point, a rotten apple lobbed into our fort, landing right on top of Paul's head. Apple juice seeped through his hair and dripped down over his face.

Sure enough, the two sides were dividing their shots between us and each other. It looked like the Clintons were getting the worst of it, by far.

"What do we do now?" I asked. Paul was trying to scrape rotten apple out of his hair. I looked over the fort shields. Young Matthew was on the ground on his elbows and knees, his face on the ground. The fingers of both hands were interlocked over the back of his head. Apples were bulleting around him. Suddenly I got an idea. "Hey, Matthew!" I shouted down to him.

"What do you want, Hawk?" he shouted back, keeping his head where it was.

"Do you guys know where our underground hut is?"

I made out a muffled "yes."

"Then head for it," I yelled. "Get your brothers and head on down the embankment. We'll follow."

Then, turning to Paul, I asked, "Are you with us?"

"I'm sure not staying here by myself," he returned.

Jerry caught a rotten apple on the left side of his face.

Paul suddenly took command again. "You guys go together again on the rope. Aim it over the embankment. I'll go down the fire pole. I'll meet you at the underground hut."

"HEY, MATTHEW," I CRIED, "DO YOU KNOW WHERE OUR UNDERGROUND HUT IS?"

THE RATS RIMMED THE RIDGE AND PELTED US UNMERCIFULLY.

Paul was first away. He went down the pole so fast I wondered if his hands were on it. The Clintons were tumbling down the embankment head over heels in their haste to reach the underground hut.

Paul leapt off the ridge, landed on his side, and rolled the rest of the way down the embankment. The Rats lined the rim, sending a hail of rotten apples pelting down on the unprotected heads below. Jerry and I grabbed the rope swing and took it as far to the rear of the fort as we could to get a good takeoff. "Are we ready?" Jerry said.

"Yeah," I said. "Let's do it."

We had a nice swing, each of us taking one of the Rats over the rim as we went, planting our feet squarely on their backs. At the height of the rope's swing, we let go. It was a hard landing as we rolled and tumbled down the embankment, but we were covering ground fast — catching up with Paul. The seven of us continued down the hill as rotten apples sliced about us. Scratch caught a good one on the back of his head. The Rat River Bunch were hot on our heels.

Hitting the meadow, we ran for our lives across the field, waded across Ca-

meron Creek, and lit out on the other side. The Rats were close behind us, still firing the occasional apple. Now they were out for blood. They really wanted to get their hands on us.

Matthew stumbled and fell, and Jerry went back for him, hoisted him to his feet, and, holding his hand, hauled him along at something approaching the speed of sound. Bypassing the swamp, we sped along the south field.

Lard Clinton got to the underground hut first. He unbolted the lock and threw the hatch open and slid down the hole like a woodchuck. Paul was there, a close second, and he disappeared down the hole, too. Ebon and Scratch

were next. I followed them and finally Matthew and Jerry, feet first, joined us. Jerry pulled the hatch down.

"Don't lock it from the inside," Paul panted. "Let them follow us. We'll go out the escape tunnel. We'll lock that hatch from the outside. It'll buy us some time."

Starting to crawl into the escape tunnel, he turned at its mouth and said, "If we hold them up in there, we can make it to the woods and split for home."

As we were crawling along, one behind the other, Uncle Thaddeus, the Clintons' little pig, was busy on the ridge, peacefully eating up all the apples.

It was dark and dank in the underground passage. We crawled through the tunnel on our hands and knees, moving as fast as we could. There was

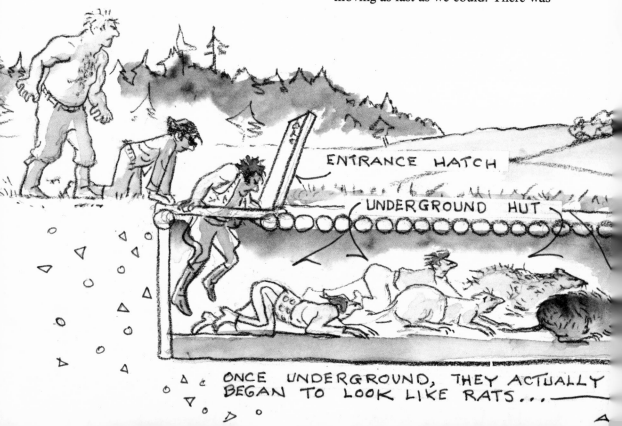

ENTRANCE HATCH

UNDERGROUND HUT

ONCE UNDERGROUND, THEY ACTUALLY BEGAN TO LOOK LIKE RATS...

some heavy breathing and a cough now and then. Scratch was just in front of me. If he hadn't been on our side now, I'd have given him a swack on the rear to speed him up.

We heard the front hatch open behind us. One by one, the Rats slipped down behind us like . . . rats. And one by one, our group crawled up into the light again. Paul stood by the hatch counting: one, two, three, four, five, six, seven; and when the last had finally surfaced outside, he slammed the hatch shut and bolted it.

"Now," he shouted, "Let's head for the woods."

ESCAPE TUNNEL

NANCY WAS DOING A LITTLE
DANCE ON THE HATCH.

"Why?" said Jerry. He was pointing
to Nancy, who had suddenly appeared
from nowhere — just in time to slam
the bolt closed at the other end. She was
doing a little dance on the hatch cover
and waving at us.

The Rats were buried alive. Both
hatches were now locked on the outside. Paul bellowed down the smoke
hole, "See you guys tomorrow, or maybe next week, or maybe next year.
Goodnight, Rats."

Then we all went home, had supper,
and climbed into bed. And all but one
fell asleep. In the middle of the night,
Nancy got up.

She put on her clothes and dropped out of her ground-floor window. Half walking and half trotting, she made her way to Christian Hollow. The moon was high over the south field and glowed with fall's night magic. She unbolted both the hatches and hurried home.

THE END

CONSULTANTS:
Paul Galloway — Contractor
Jerry Galloway — Contractor
Judith Hayward — Educator
Trafford Hicks — Engineer
Earl Kathan — Contractor
John Stevens — Former Mate: Sail and Steam

About the Author and His Friends:

Austin Stevens grew up in Walpole, New Hampshire. He studied art at the Boston Museum School of Fine Art and graduated from Tufts University in 1956. Austin has been writing and illustrating for books and magazines for 25 years. He is married and the father of two grown children. Paul Galloway is today a very successful contractor. Paul and Austin still live in Walpole and still just about a mile apart. Nancy (Galloway) Drohan is married and the mother of 4 children. She lives in Nashua, New Hampshire. Jerry Hamill moved to Mexico in 1953 and started his own business. But nobody knows where the Clinton brothers went.